CW00421668

RO-ᴚᴜ
TO FINLAND

By Barry Mitchell

HUTTON PRESS
1985

Hutton Press Ltd.
130 Canada Drive, Cherry Burton, Beverley
North Humberside HU17 7SB

Printed by Clifford Ward & Co.
(Bridlington) Ltd.
55 West Street, Bridlington, East Yorkshire
YO15 3DZ

ISBN 0 907033 32 6

ACKNOWLEDGEMENTS

First and foremost I am indebted to the generosity and foresight of Mr. H. Castenskiold, Managing Director of the United Baltic Corporation. At all times my requests for access to m.v. 'Baltic Enterprise' were met with his fullest cooperation. Without assistance of this nature there would have been no book.

I am also indebted to all the seagoing and shore staff of U.B.C. who consciously or unconsciously have helped in compiling this work. Several are mentioned within the text but there are many more who have made equally important contributions. It would be difficult to individually name each and every person who, over the period of my involvement with the U.B.C. operation, have offered a wealth of information. To all of them I wish to express my sincere thanks.

I would, however, like to take the opportunity to individually thank Captain Gerald Brazendale for his cooperation both at sea and ashore, not the least in reading through the manuscript and giving invaluable advice.

Further my gratitude for help received extends to Mr. Frank Berry, Operations Manager of the Humber Pilots; Humber Pilot John Ashby; Ms. Jane Ashford, Dunelm Public Relations Ltd.; The Docks Manager, Associated British Ports, Hull; Captain Claes Soderholm, Finland Steamship Company; Oy Finncarriers Ab, Helsinki.

Cover illustration from a watercolour by G. F. Overton, Bridlington.

INTRODUCTION

The economics of present-day shipping rely heavily upon the most effective cargo handling systems and the speed at which these systems can be employed to discharge and reload a waiting ship. The techniques used to effect such efficiency require specialised types of ships that are far removed from the vessels that were the norm less than a generation ago.

Particularly on the short-sea routes the roll-on roll-off principle of handling cargo has revolutionised the industry. To deploy this system purpose-built roll-on roll-off vessels (ro-ro ships as they have become known) arrived on the scene. They are so designed as to enable an entire cargo to be driven aboard on wheels. Often these ships are elusive to the landsman — adhering to stringent sailing schedules the ro-ro spends but a few hours in turn-round; thus time to assess these vessels while in port is very limited. In addition the berths that they use are frequently remote from the public. Other than those professionally involved few people have the chance to take a good look at these ships let alone have the opportunity to step aboard and sense the mood of urgency under which they operate. It is hoped that in some way this book will help to bridge that gap.

Obviously in order to describe its mode of operation and see the way of life of the men who crew it one has to sail aboard such a vessel. This book is a product of three round voyages aboard m.v. 'Baltic Enterprise' which was owned and operated by the United Baltic Corporation, London. The initial voyage was made with the sole intention of writing a short magazine article about the U.K.-Finland service on which this ro-ro ship operated. On publication the article attracted a great deal of response both from home and overseas readers. Much of the mail was in request for further details and information about the ship and the journey.

'Ro-Ro to Finland' came as a natural follow-up, but in order to compile this work I found a further two voyages necessary. The text is based on the second of the three. However each journey unveiled new information and provided varied events and sightings. To obtain the fullest coverage of the service and to add to the enjoyment of the reader I have fused this comprehensive detail into the text. Therefore without detracting from the authenticity of the operation the result is to a lesser degree in the nature of a composite voyage.

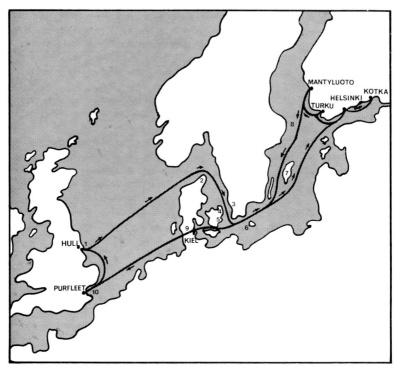

The 11-day, 2,900-mile circuit. Along with the six ports of call, the ship sailed close to the shores of five different countries. Some strategic points en route: 1, Spurn Point (U.K.); 2, Skagen and The Skaw (Denmark); 3, Halsingborg (Sweden); 4, Helsingor; 5, Copenhagen; 6, Bornholm (Denmark); 7, Gotland (Sweden); 8, Aland Islands (Finland); 9, Kiel Canal and River Elbe (W. Germany); 10, Sunk Lightship.

'Baltic Enterprise,' 4,667 gross tons (5,600 deadweight tons), length 452ft., breadth 73ft., speed 18½ knots.

6

CHAPTER ONE

With radar aerials energetically rotating, flags tugging at their haliyards and a plume of black exhaust smoke lifting from her warm funnel, 'Baltic Enterprise' was in no way attempting to conceal the fact that she was a ship about to put to sea. The massive doors at her stern, which throughout the day had formed a horizontal bridge for an incessant perambulation of cargo, were secured bolt upright. Towering surprisingly high above her maindeck they had transformed her hull into an impregnable steel fortress. The sheen from their grey painted shells gently reflected the orange sunlight back westwards across a now deserted concrete loading ramp.

Apart from the six bar-taut mooring lines that spreadeagled downwards from her maindeck fairleads the ship had severed all physical contact with the shore. Deceptively dwarfed by the great high-rise slab of her starboard side the men who attended the quayside mooring bollards were last in line of a small army of people who had toiled throughout the day's oppressive heat to effect the ship's turn-round. The clamour that had engulfed the vessel during that operation had subsided to a faint whisper — closed were the doors of the surrounding transit sheds — gone was the train of unitised cargo that had flowed from them — garaged was the vehicular apparatus that had relentlessly chugged and groaned to feed it into the ship's hungry belly. Remaining evidence of the dismissed procession was confined to tell-tale scraps of refuse that lay around the dusty dockside.

This cessation of waterside activity marked the prelude to a July weekend which for many held the promise of a couple of relaxed carefree days. But for 'Baltic Enterprise' and her crew it marked the commencement of another chapter in an encyclopaedia of voyages between the shores of Britain and Finland. Measuring 4667 gross tons 'Enterprise' was one of the modern generation of roll-on roll-off cargo ferries termed in shipping circles as a 'ro-ro.' Owned by the London-based United Baltic Corporation she operated together with sister ship 'Baltic Progress' on a specialised 'high speed' U.K./Finland service. Two further identical vessels, 'Orion' and 'Sirius' owned by the Finland Steamship Company of Helsinki, were involved. The combined operation was a partnership of the two companies known as Oy Finanglia Ferries Ltd.

'Baltic Enterprise's' latest homeward voyage had terminated at the Humber port of Hull in the early hours of that morning. Having discharged 4,000 tons of unitised general cargo before mid-day she had reloaded with an equal capacity of British exports in readiness for her scheduled 19.30 departure to Helsinki.

Now, with main engines turning, she was obediently waiting her turn to enter the huge lock that would facilitate her release from the Queen Elizabeth Dock to the River Humber.

Aboard her I had entered an environment of fitted carpets and lounge chairs, of sophisticated electronic instruments and modest profes-sionalism, of lavish meals and technically biased conversation, of containers, trailers, lashing chains and engines. The mood generated there was that which a small self-contained community adopts while in the throes of briefly detaching itself from the turmoil of landward life.

Amid the dockwater's excited ripples and presiding over the lockpit entrance at that very time was the Rotterdam-bound giant car-passenger ferry 'Norland.' Many of her 1,100 passengers lined the decks to witness the skills of the master in coaxing her 12,988 gross ton mass through the lock's open jaws. For several moments, as the ferry angled in the breeze, doubts were raised as to the feasibility of the exercise. However, with variable pitch screws churning a maelstrom of brown water to check her sideways momentum, the largest Hull registered ship crawled forward until with barely nine inches clearance at either side, she was encompassed within the grey walls. Eight miles down river was one of 'Norland's' smaller sister ships — 'Norwind.' She had negotiated the lock thirty minutes earlier and was by then stemming the Humber flood tide at sixteen knots towards the open sea and her morning goal — Zeebrugge. Since inaugurating their services with one ship in 1965 the operators, North Sea Ferries, had invested heavily to create a motorway to Europe system in each direction seven days a week.

Ferries like these paved the way for the ro-ro principle to become an accepted means of handling general cargo. It was realised that the facility of high-speed turn-rounds was becoming an essential factor in the economics of short-sea operations. Thus in the early 70's many conventional freighters were phased out in favour of the cargo-on-wheels principle. In a profession where old traditions die hard the ro-ro ship has appraised unanimous acclaim. They have not just brought ship-board comforts to a standard unimagined only a couple of decades ago but also a whole new lifestyle to those who crew them.

While pondering at 'Enterprise's' after rail it seemed fitting that I should be commencing a voyage aboard this new generation of ship at Hull. Being traditionally a seaman's town it has borne the wind of change that for seven-hundred years has persistently blown across its waterside activities. The quiet waters that confronted me circumscribed the present maritime element there and also reflected the traumatic days gone by.

Though there is evidence that Hull existed more than one hundred years earlier it is generally accepted that Edward I was the founder in 1293. During a hunting holiday in the area he was invited to inspect a growing port that was situated at the confluence of the River Hull with the Humber. Being impressed with what he saw he named it Kings Town upon Hull. Over the following centuries, Hull, as it became more economically called, has had periods of vast development and prosperity together with times of dire hardship and depression.

Various charters have been granted to Hull and as early as 1440 it became one of the first towns in the country. In 1541, realising the importance of the port, Henry the Eighth ordered that all existing fortifications should be strengthened. Apart from having a castle and blockhouses built he had movable chains stretched across the mouth of the River Hull.

Between 1422 and 1637 the town's progress was intermittently interrupted through several outbreaks of the plague that ultimately caused the deaths of thousands of people. In the 18th and 19th centuries the port flourished once more. During that time fine commercial premises sprang up and a maze of docks and warehouses extended right into the town. With ocean-going vessels berthed hard-up against the main thoroughfares, Hull, despite its riverside situation, had the air of a salt-sea town. By the time Queen Victoria had conferred the title of City to the township in 1897 the docks extended in both directions along the Humber shores.

In World War I German submarines continually hampered Humber shipping while at the same time airships bombed the docks and town. Unfortunately this was only a foretaste of the misery yet to come for twenty-one years later Hull was again one of the main targets of the enemy. Only those who lived in and around the city at that time can have any idea of the onslaught caused by German bombers. Thousands were killed or injured when of 92,000 houses only 600 escaped damage. On top of this Hull's commercial premises were progressively levelled from endless raids of incendiary and explosive bombs. There were tremendous fires and incalculable damage was done. Throughout the Germans had to be kept in ignorance of the injuries they were inflicting upon the port so it was only after the hostilities had ceased that anything could be published about it.

In the recovery years after the war Hull's deep-sea fishing industry was at its peak — the commercial docks were equally thronged. Today the situation has completely reversed itself. International policital sanctions have totally decimated Hull's future as a fishing port and, at the same juncture, where commercial shipping used to be the town's lifeblood it has progressively dwindled to became an integral segment of its varied industrial assets. Now the old 'Town Docks' are closed. They had neither enough water, the right kind of storage or adequate access to accommodate the ever-increasing size of 20th century ships. Consequently they fell into disuse. One, Queen's Dock, was filled in and became an ornamental garden with a central promenade. The others remain empty but there is a programme to develop them as yacht marinas and leisure centres.

Hull's condensed 'new look' shipping activities are concentrated on the deep-water King George and Queen Elizabeth Docks which broach the north bank of the Humber three miles east of the city centre.

Having, that Friday afternoon, driven past the ripening cornfields of the Holderness Plain, through the unimaginative East Hull suburbs and along the $1\frac{1}{2}$ mile arm of Queen Elizabeth Dock I had stopped my car in the long low shadow of No. 15 transit shed. There was good reason to halt there for as well as running out of road I had arrived at the embarkation place for the Scandinavian voyage.

Whether seen at sea or in port the stern view of a ro-ro ship is unlikely to stir one into a stupor of admiration. Indeed for anyone with an eye to beauty it is a vista that would not justify a second glance. In simple terms an abruptly squared-off hull blocked by a door fit to guard a strongroom offers little to enhance a ship's external features. With two such doors hinged side by side across her generous 73 foot beam 'Baltic Enterprise' was no exception — it was this uncompromising aspect of the ship that greeted me on rounding the corner of the transit shed. Resting prone onto a wide concrete ramp these heavy doors were yawning an open invitation to a fleet of trailer-burdened tractors that perpetually dashed about the adjacent quayside. Suitcase in hand I continued through the noise and bustle of that busy concourse towards the sundrenched loading ramp. There a young fair-haired officer, who had identified me as one of seven passengers due to embark for the imminent voyage, approached to lead the way.

The route on which I was guided was not entirely unfamiliar. Several years earlier, following the ship's inauguration to the service, I had climbed the very same steel stairway. On that occasion I was aboard in response to an invitation to write a magazine article about the vessel. Having received much favourable mail after its publication the article proved to be an unqualified success. And yet I was aware that within its meagre 1,500 words I had hardly begun to scratch the surface of the story behind the operation. Now I was back to compile a more conclusive profile of the ship, the men who crewed her and of the varied environmental aspects of a complete round voyage. As I walked across the ship's green painted after-deck that warm summer afternoon I looked anew upon my involvement and it is in that context that I scribe the chapters of this book.

In retrospect I suppose my interest in maritime affairs began when as a seven-year-old I visited H.M.S. Anson at anchor in Torbay. It was open day and groups of people were ferried to the battleship in small open launches from Torquay harbour. While on the guided tour I had seen several gold-braided high-ranking officers resplendently strutting around the ship's immaculate decks. Afterwards I announced that I wished to conduct my future career as Admiral of the Fleet! Unfortunately not only did that distinction evade my subsequent working life but so did any other professional involvement in nautical directions. Undaunted by the circumstances that steered me away from a life at sea I adopted a compromise by settling into adult life with a position within an industrial concern at the seaside town of Bridlington. Being restricted to an occasional summertime dinghy excursion in local waters or riding-out storms with Chichester, Rose, Knox-Johnson and Blyth from a wintertime armchair my sea-going experiences have not flourished to a great extent. Yet by just living within sight and sound of the sea one senses a means of escape: a freedom from claustrophobic city streets, incessant traffic congestion and the pressures of modern living. Man's devious ways of defacing the land are totally inept when considering the oceans — it is unlikely that he will ever build factories, motorways or towerblocks there. In the passing of time ships are the only significant instruments to have been placed on its surface and yet, though modern technology has changed their appearance and character, the relentless task of gaining superiority over the sea's limitless forces continue.

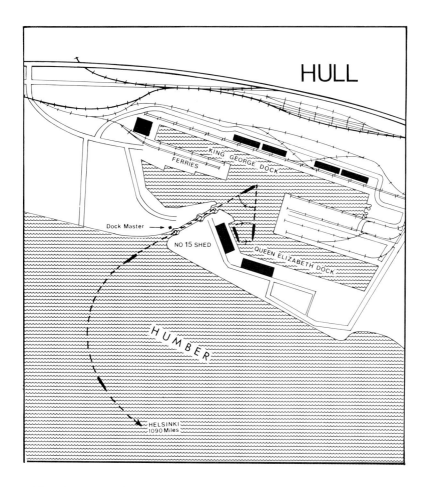

For the non-seafarer the living area of a ship in the class of 'Baltic Enterprise' is best compared to a small three-star graded hotel. Being enclosed within the main superstructure it rises three or four decks above the main hull section. It is a completely independent unit comprising every present-day amenity necessary to comfortably accommodate both crew and a small number of passengers. In providing this no corners have been cut; on first entering the accommodation block one reacts to a smartness above and beyond all expectation.

The 'hotel manager' is the Chief Steward or as more recently called the Catering Officer. He is directly responsible to the Captain for the day-to-day administration of the accommodation and catering requirements of all those aboard. Apart from handling catering accounts, ordering stores and

Opened stern doors form a double bridge system. This allows simultaneous loading/unloading.

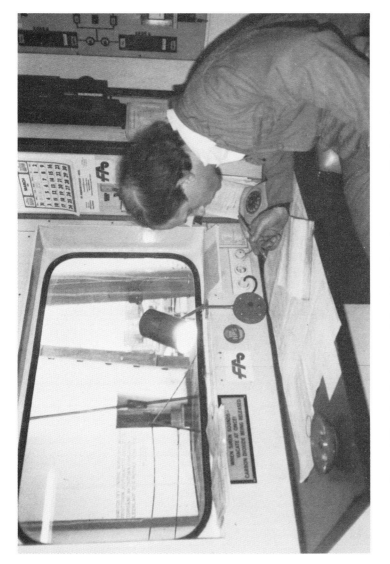

Bernard Elworthy checks cargo being driven aboard past cargo office/control room.

23-ton gantry crane loading chemical tankers onto weather deck.

14

provisions, controlling stewards and pantry boys and attending to the welfare of passengers he is usually something of a father figure within the section. The turn-round scene in the ship's tiny catering office is one of continuous formal and informal comings and goings. Operating to extremely tight sailing schedules a ro-ro vessel may have as little as six hours in her home port. Within that short period all victualling arrangements for the imminent voyage have to be carried out. Along with dealing with the formalities presented to him by Customs and Immigration officers the Catering Officer has to contract the representatives from chandlers, butchers, laundries, brewery and tobacco companies.

Aboard 'Baltic Enterprise' the Catering Officer image was amicably portrayed in the ample figure of John Garvey. In his late forties he was a man who had sailed to almost every corner of the world on ships as varied as the countries he had visited. The last sixteen years of this seagoing career had been spent with the U.B.C. company.

"You certainly didn't intend being left on the quayside." On introducing himself with a firm handshake John Garvey joked about my early embarkation.

From the after deck my guide had showed me to a veneered door along a wide alleyway on the second level of the accommodation area. Peering over the Catering Officer's shoulder I could see that on having company he was obviously in the midst of ship's business. Fortunately the visitor turned out to be the duty Immigration Officer so the usual embarkation formalities were carried out there and then. My premature arrival had been planned to allow time to see the loading procedure along with some of the shore installations and equipment which are as much a part of the ro-ro operation as the ship itself. Equally I was keen to review the ship's vital statistics from the shore as I was aware that once confined aboard at sea it would be difficult to regain the impression of her lines. Having deposited my luggage I left John Garvey to his work and hastened to retrace my steps back to the noise of the labouring tractors.

Back at the loading ramp I watched these two-hundred horsepower 'Tugmaster' vehicles haul trailer after trailer aboard the ship. Each load was individually driven onto one of the 'tween decks which were accessible from the stern doors. On entering the hollow garage-like interior, traffic for the upper 'tween deck was elevated by means of an internal ramp system and parked on one of the six lanes that were marked out along the length of the ship. Additionally at this level two opened hatches allowed containers to be lifted from their trailers and deposited on the outside weatherdeck above. This was effected by a 23-ton gantry crane that was driven on tracks forward of the superstructure. When the internal ramps were reversed across access was gained to the lower 'tween deck which was also six traffic lanes wide. A pair of 45-ton lifts at this deck level were used to move cargo to a lower hold with approximately half the capacity of one of the 'tween decks. Together the four cargo decks provided space for 288 units of the 20 foot size or an equivalent amount of 40 foot units with room to spare for a variety of vehicles such as lorries, tractors, cars or caravans. The loading process was fascinating to watch. From my safe vantage point it appeared that no matter how many units were 'rolled' aboard, the ship consumed them without any undue congestion.

Enjoying the warmth of the summer day I later strolled the dockside beneath the 452 foot length of the ship. Along there I passed neatly parked agricultural tractors and fearsome looking excavators that were about to be loaded. Soon I was in a position to establish that, like most ships, 'Enterprise' was at her visual best when viewed at an angle to the bow. Here the overall impact was size. In present-day terms her modest sounding gross tonnage suggested a relatively small vessel, but gazing at the U.B.C. motif crowning her towering forepeak one could have been excused, as it was later suggested, for taking her for a ship of 12,000 gross tons. Flaring aftwards from her bows, raised to the height of a house from the water with a minimal amount of sheer and being totally unbroken by port holes, the formidable walls of her hull created a striking impression of bulk. In silhouette from the opposite shore 'Enterprise' could have been seen as a scaled-down tanker or bulk carrier for, added above the cliff-like walls of her hull, her main superstructure sited almost aft was somewhat characteristic of that belonging to the giants that ply between the oil terminals of the world. Agreed, most of her lines were either horizontal or perpendicular. She decidedly lacked the graceful contours familiar in the tonnage of yesteryear but, in fairness, the innumerable multi-coloured containers that were being continually stacked along the expanse of her weatherdeck were steadily contributing towards this angular appearance. The very essence of unit load transportation is in the squaring-off of each cargo unit by stowing inside containers onto slave trailers. In submission to the proverb 'You can't fit a square peg into a round hole' angular cargoes require angular ships to transport them!

It would not be true to fact to claim 'Baltic Enterprise' as a typical ro-ro freighter yet, on the other hand, it would be difficult to say exactly what characteristics define a typical ship of this class — like human beings they come in all shapes and sizes. Each ship is purpose-built to fulfill a specialised role but having the one common factor — the ability to accept an entire cargo on wheels. It would seem, however, that the majority of short-sea ro-ro operators favour a vessel similar in stature to a road lorry — driving compartment up front and load behind. Basically this design provides for a totally unobstructed forward vista from the bridge together with the facility of driving cargo directly onto the weatherdeck as well as the normal 'tween decks from the stern ramps. These advantages are balanced against a number of contrasting disadvantages into which I will look later in this book.

It is unlikely that any ro-ro vessel could be more purpose-built than the 'Baltic' ships. Yet in retaining the main superstructure at the after end of the hull the marine architects have happily upheld a basic traditional image. By displaying a squat cream-painted funnel 'Enterprise' scored well against many of her contemporaries — here reed-like uprake exhausts poking from the extremities of a ship's quarters have become the rule rather than the exception. In turn, to her advantage, neither did her gleaming white superstructure rise like a city towerblock; its stepped sides, furnished with motorised lifeboats, were progressively flanked with wide orchard green decks. In summary, considering she was a pure ro-ro freighter, 'Baltic Enterprise' outwardly displayed a certain distinctive styling. Whether it was this unpretentious, yet individualistic, appearance or otherwise simply because I was aware the vessel was to be my mentor for the next nine days I do not know, but the more I contemplated her, the more favourably I looked upon her functional lines.

While the present-day purchase of a freighter in this class involves an investment in the order of £10 million the day-to-day operating costs are equally phenomenal. Fuel, insurance, maintenance, wages, food, pilotage and harbour dues combine to evoke overheads that would stagger the man in the street. Not surprisingly ships are operated on the principle that they are too costly to be kept still. Every hour spent idle whilst waiting a berth or wasted in the handling of difficult cargoes weighs heavily on the debit side of the balance sheets. On this account the age of the unit load arrived as more of an economic necessity than as a novel mode of sea transportation. In this respect where a conventional freighter employed on short-sea trading can spend upwards of 60% of the year at the dockside a ro-ro ship on the same trade would not be expected to be immobile more than 25% of the year.

During an earlier visit to Hull these facts and figures were made clear to me by U.B.C. Port Captain Chris Woodall. On that occasion I was shown over two conventional cargo ships berthed in the now closed Alexandra Dock. Fresh from dry dock 'Baltic Venture' was about to be loaded with general cargo for the Polish port of Gdynia while at the opposite quay, sitting on her load line with 3,400 tons aboard, 'Baltic Valiant' was ready to depart on her regular service to Leningrad. I was told that 'Valiant' had arrived from the Russian port similarly burdened nine days earlier. The lengthy turn-round had resulted from the handling and stowing of myriad items of individual cargo. Related to a ro-ro system the vessel could have been heading back to sea with the same amount of cargo within twelve hours.

"In principle the ro-ro system allows the ship's decks to be prepared in the transit sheds before the turn-round day," Woodall explained. "All items of freight — textiles, building materials, feeding stuffs, machinery, fertilisers, plastics or vehicle parts for example — are pre-loaded onto slave trailers or into containers before the ship arrives. On berthing it's 'all systems go,' first unlashing the incoming loaded trailers from the ship's decks, hauling them ashore to the intake bays then reversing the procedure with the export freight."

Working on and around 'Baltic Enterprise' that hot July afternoon were eighteen dockers and fourteen riggers. Their labours of driving and securing aboard the 3,800 tons of outward cargo was the culmination of three days work involving some sixty employees at the Hull base of the Finanglia operation. At the quayside amidst the fervour, the lithe bearded figure of Chris Woodall was much in evidence. Directing the loading operation was a job that kept him on the move — on foot, bicycle or further afield in a white estate car that displayed the Finanglia emblem. Such was his mobility it was some time before I was able to pin him down to renew our acquaintance; even then our meeting was brief. The reverberating noise of the chugging Tugmasters made conversation uphill work but in all I gathered that he was more than satisfied with the turn-round.

"Things have run quite smoothly today — no labour problems, breakdowns or bad weather — another hour should see the job completed," he shouted.

He made it clear that in maintaining a ro-ro vessel on its exacting schedules there was always the fickle human, mechanical and climatic temperaments to contend with. Woodall, that day, had been spared any of these impeding troubles yet, until the last of the twenty tons of chains that lashed the cargo to the ship's decks were fixed, he was to continue to have the mark of a man under pressure. The persistent diligence he applied to the situation was spelled out as he moved off with lengthy strides towards the office phone.

It was time to re-embark. Under the ro-ro's starboard quarter which was embellished at the rim with large black letters bearing BALTIC ENTERPRISE, LONDON, I took a final assessment of her vast hull. The gauge there showed that she was drawing slightly more than nineteen feet of water and yet, on gazing aloft, it seemed that the 3,800 tons now aboard had accomplished nothing towards belittling her soaring freeboard. Adding my meagre twelve stones to that load was not going to make any impression either; in fact it would be about as undetected as a fly on a freight train or a moth on a monster lorry — I hastened to the ramp least I should be forgotten!

CHAPTER TWO

On re-boarding the ship I found that my luggage had been placed on a rack in one of the two main forward facing passenger cabins, a seat awaiting me at the centre table in the dining saloon and a quick introduction to several of the ship's company who were dashing away to their respective stations. My first meal aboard was a hurried affair with the imminent departure taking preferential interest over what appeared to be a well-balanced menu of wholesome English food. Everyone seemed to have somewhere to go or something to do, consequently it was not long before I too joined the exodus from the U.B.C. inscribed tableware. I had been invited to the bridge — moreover to see 'Enterprise' manoeuvred from her berth, through the lock pit and piloted the twenty-two miles down river to the sea. Therefore a tightly sprung door at the head of a short inside stairway that led from the main accommodation area was my objective.

Entering the bridgehouse I was confronted by a spread of consoles massed with banks of multi-coloured switches, knobs, dials and levers creating a scene that could have been taken straight from a space control centre. They were lined two-thirds the width of the silent interior beneath nine angled windows that overlooked the weatherdeck twenty-five feet below. To the rear of this scrupulously tidy control room was a screened-off area containing chart tables, chronometers, drawers and desks where entries in the ship's log were made. Directly in the centre, rising from the carpeted deck, was a plinth shouldering the rudder direction indicator, the gyro compass display together with the ship's wheel — if it could be called a wheel! This was a semi-circular affair similar to those seen in an aircraft cockpit. Latched to it were the hands of a swarthy able-seaman who, waiting orders, stood reverently with eyes firmly glued to the instruments before him. At each end of the fifty-five foot wide bridgehouse was a lavishly varnished sliding door that provided access to the open bridge wings that crept out to overlook the ship's sides.

Assembled on the starboard wing were the Master of 'Baltic Enterprise,' Captain Gerald Brazendale — he was in his mid-forties, was stockily built and had a good head of hair that tended to fall over his forehead; the ship's Chief Officer, Peter Green, who was a lean six-footer of thirty years of age; and finally Humber Pilot John Ashby, a man in his late forties who was content in taking a back seat until the ship was manipulated into the river.

While peering over the side the Captain was issuing orders into a portable radio telephone that was strapped over his shoulder. (This is a vital form of communication between bridge and mooring decks on present-day ships).

In response to his commands, fore and aft crews, who had been called to their stations earlier, began to haul aboard the heavy warps that one by one were being loosened from the quay bollards by shorehands. Hands hovering over the engine controls, Captain Brazendale craned his head back and forth calmly waiting for the moment the ship would be completely detached from the wharfe.

Bridgehouse interior. The ship's wheel is on the left of the picture.

20

Commencing a voyage to Finland – entering the lock at Hull.

An important characteristic of a ro-ro ship is that under normal weather conditions it is equipped to manoeuvre in and out of port without the assistance of tugs. This has been arranged by dispensing with the age-old telegraph system between bridge and engine room. Instead, the master has direct control over the engines both from the main fascia in the bridge-house and duplicate controls sited at the extremities of each wing. These neat twin (inverted 'L' shaped) levers not only govern the power transmitted to the propellers but also control the amount of pitch inclined upon them. For range of pitch and power each lever is calibrated through an arc from zero to ten both ahead and astern. A further and most essential innovation towards independent handling is the bow thrust propeller. Set deep in the water at right angles to the hull this electrically driven screw can be operated at variable speeds either to port or starboard effectually giving the provision of a small tug working at the bows.

Within the confines of Queen Elizabeth Dock, 'Baltic Enterprise' appeared a ship of considerable size — this few would dispute. Even at that time, with a number of vacant berths, space to move a vessel almost half the length of Q.E.2 was not excessive. The exercise of taking her safely from the Finland Terminal to the lock pit was entirely dependant upon the expertise of the Master in handling the main engine controls and in his calculated commands to the seaman at the wheel.

Motioning Chief Officer Peter Green to his side, Brazendale nonchalantly brought in the starboard engine to three ahead. Meanwhile Green hung onto a button below the white side coaming to effect a long bellowing siren blast that panicked countless gulls from the dock area. At this stage, at a snail's pace, the ship began to slide forward.

'Enterprise' had been moored starboard side to the quay with her stern firmly butted against the wide concrete ramp. Ahead, slightly angled across her bow at No.14 berth, lay a conventional freighter of around 5,000 gross tons. There were approximately twenty-five yards of clear water between the two vessels. The lock basin towards which she had to be headed was directly astern sited at ninety degrees to the ro-ro berth. In the exercise of presenting her bows to the lock jaws she had to be pulled away from the quay for a number of yards in almost a crabwise manner. This would create sufficient clearance for the stern to be swung out at forty-five degrees. Situated thus there would be enough clear water to enable her to be taken astern about three ship lengths — turning tightly a further forty-five degrees to starboard to give a direct heading for the seemingly narrow opening.

The R.T. squawked out a message from Second Officer Bernard Elworthy positioned on the aft mooring deck to the effect that there was sufficient clearance astern for the ship to be pulled away. Brazendale worked at the controls — three astern starboard engine, four ahead port engine and bow thrust half speed to starboard — and expectantly returned his gaze to the quay edge. Hesitantly the forward crawl ceased giving way to a detectable sideways motion that gradually opened up a narrow moat between the two walls.

The Captain's opening moves had been orchestrated purely as a tentative measure because, pushing against the port side, the fresh evening breeze was tending to hold the ship to the quay heading. Having tested her stride against this encumbrance he whisked the controls into a wider gate — six astern starboard, six ahead port and bow thrust full speed to starboard. In almost immediate response to this directive the ship awoke from her leisurely attitude into a burst of energy. Stirring one's ear-drums the funnel-top exhausts broke out from the relaxed murmuring into a heavy rhythmic bark thrusting skywards a volley of soot-speckled clouds. Deep down, the large screws, opposing each other in the laborious task of drawing the laden ship from the staging, bit furiously at the brown water inducing spasmodic bouts of quavering vibration to dissipate through the hull. Widening, the moat became a river — a river of swirling opaque liquid escaping from a seething cauldron beneath the stern.

"When we have a wind of over force five in this direction we have to call for a tug to give a helping hand," Brazendale called over to me as I observed him opening the respective engine controls to eight in each direction and cutting the bow thrust. Keeping a low profile while the Captain concentrated on the ship's progress, I gave a cursory acknowledgement to his statement. Later I was to learn that when the wind reaches that strength swirling across the dock a good deal of turbulance is stirred up. Apart from the tremendous pressure against the ship's port side, freak eddies are created resulting in the vessel being able to move but a few yards off the quay then being held there. Regardless of what ratio of power is applied, the ship refuses to move.

"Hard to starboard!" Brazendale called in full voice.

"Hard to starboard!" came the customary verbal response from the steersman at the wheel.

With the stern swinging out with increasing speed, Peter Green sited himself on the port wing to act as blind-side look-out. There was no doubt, judging from the contentment on Brazendale's face, that up to now the manoeuvre was going strictly to plan.

Remaining unobtrusive during his wait, Pilot Ashby paced to and fro across the wing duckboarding, firstly watching the action from the rail and then from the bridgehouse, intermittently glancing at his wrist watch obviously in calculating the state of the tide.

Although the Pilot is nominally in charge of the vessel from the time it has been cast off until it reaches the river mouth, it is accepted that on a ro-ro ship the Captain will conduct the close manoeuvring within the dock. It could not be expected of anyone to jump into the driving seat of a vehicle which he does not handle on a regular basis and manipulate it with the dexterity of one who is well practised.

Drawing his attention I questioned John Ashby on this point. "All conventional ships have to use tugs to take them to the river," he explained. "The Pilot always takes full control of this operation. With ro-ro ships not using tugs things are a little different — each has its own whims which require time and space to master. Usually the Captain prefers to take the controls and we have no objection to this arrangement," he added. "The one exception is in the case of Russian ro-ro's. Surprisingly all Masters of these ships ask the Pilot to handle the whole operation. Normally one or two arrive here each week so we are not entirely without ro-ro driving experience!"

Scanning the now empty berth, our bow momentarily pointed at Chris Woodall, arms folded and leaning against his car, the U.B.C. Port Captain had finally adopted a stationary posture to watch the ship make its exit. For him it was the wind-up to a hectic week and the start of a two-day break. Come Monday the Finnish ship 'Sirius' would be arriving to occupy the berth and every minute of his time.

Of the four identical ro-ro's operating on Finanglia Ferries services, two, 'Baltic Enterprise' and 'Sirius,' sailed on a regular basis out of Hull. One ship covered the South Coast of Finland, first calling at the capital, Helsinki, and then on to Kotka — an industrial centre some ninety miles to the east. The other ship made for the West Coast of Finland, taking in Turku, a major ferry port, and then moved a hundred miles north to a remote port with an appropriate far-sounding name — Mantyluoto. Heading back to England the ship on the latter did not return to Hull. Instead, using the Kiel Canal to cut down the distance, it carried on to London or to be more precise a ro-ro terminal at Purfleet, which is situated on the North Bank of the Thames.

Of the other two vessels, 'Baltic Progress' maintained a regular seven-day service out of Purfleet to Helsinki and 'Orion' held a sailing out of Felixstowe every Friday to Turku and Kotka.

To all intents and purposes we were departing on the Hull-South Finland service. However there was to be an interesting diversion on the return voyage. Once a year, in order to comply with the Lloyds classification survey, each vessel was taken in turn out of service for two weeks dry-docking. At that particular time 'Baltic Progress' was dry-docked thus leaving her capital to capital run to be temporarily covered by the other ships. While on our scheduled call at Helsinki we were to take aboard some London-bound cargo. On completing our Finnish loading at Kotka the re-routing was to take us through the Kiel Canal directly to the Purfleet base. On return from the Thames to Hull we would have sailed close on three thousand miles, half of which would be close by the coastlines of five different countries.

The whole process of manoeuvring the burdened ro-ro from its snug sanctuary to the open sea for this voyage was a ritual of persuasion by a team of twelve men — four on the bridge, six manning the fore and aft mooring decks and two deep down in the engine room watching over the banks of dials and gauges that issue performance readings from the entanglement of thudding machinery down there. Undoubtedly Gerry Brazendale was the chief administrator — his fleeting adjustments to the engines came without contemplation or hesitation as were his terse commands to the man at the wheel. They had to be for the first stage of the route was a restricted one. Any indication of the ship straying from it had to be instantly detected and arrested. An anomaly of these ships is that they can receive more than a favourable push from the wind against their enormous freeboard one minute then have to reluctantly heave into it the next. This can never be overlooked. Unchecked momentum in such confines could cause vast damage both to the offending vessel and other ships or shore installations within. To a landsman adapted to an everyday vista of high-speed traffic, the manoeuvre would have appeared a slow motion business, it was — it had to be.

Brazendale turned his head towards the bridgehouse doorway — "Midships!"

"Midships," bounced back at him from the shaded depths.

Having run sideways and astern from her berth, 'Enterprise' had screwed through ninety degrees to face the lock. Now with both engines at two ahead she was making forward way with an agreeable smoothness.

Being a watercourse subject to a massive tidal surge, the Humber often produces a rise and fall in excess of twenty feet. Consequently lock gates between river and dock are an essential feature at all Humber ports. Without gates to retain a constant level within, a ship would spend half the day immobile on the dock bottom. Such conditions would not favour a roll-on roll-off operation. For example, in urgent circumstances, when through mechanical fault or industrial dispute the lock gates at Queen Elizabeth Dock have been closed, it had been attempted to load these ships while moored to the river side of the dock wall. After working three hours over high tide the stern ramps became too steeply inclined to continue. Fortunately essential items of cargo were turned round and the ship was able to maintain its schedule.

The lock-pit into which we were headed serves both King George and Queen Elizabeth Docks. Opened in 1914 it can accommodate ships up to 750 feet in length and 85 feet beam. Having secondary gates approximately one-third of the way along its length, the water capacity can be greatly reduced, helping smaller ships to be worked through more quickly.

After 'Norland' had been lowered to the river, the outer gates had been closed, the pit reflooded and the main inner gates opened for our entrance. The operation of sluicing the lock into the river has little or no effect on the water level of the ninety acres of dock that it serves. A nearby pumphouse ducted to the river is geared to feed back and maintain a constant level.

From high up on the bridge, as our bow nudged between the stone piers, the ship appeared considerably wider than the distance across the pit. However when, inch by inch, foot by foot, Gerry Brazendale edged her between the yawning inner gates the illusion subsided. In fact 'Enterprise' blocked the lock width for all but twelve feet — this our Captain distributed three at the starboard (mooring) side and nine to port. In concentric movements he would turn to scan along the hull checking against any deviation in the parallel run to the piers. Seventy-three feet away, Peter Green in likewise manner was keeping the same vigil over the port wing. Then in response to what seemed an inaudible message through a V.H.F. loudspeaker, Pilot Ashby broke off a quiet verbal exchange with Gerry Brazendale to move into the bridgehouse. There, dark glasses pushed onto his forehead, the uniformed Pilot issued a progress report through a hand microphone to the controller at the Spurn Point Pilot Station. Meanwhile, retaining his fixed stare at the rudder direction indicator, the seaman at the wheel seemed totally oblivious to this intrusion of the bridgehouse quiet.

Ships taking their leave have always attracted a variety of onlookers. Often they are relatives or loved ones of those aboard. Some are there purely to satisfy their own curiosity, yet others are sentimentalists to whom the occasion holds an irresistible magnetism.

Few though they were at the lock side that summer evening the ship gazers there seemed to fit into such mentioned groups. And to them, with her battleship-grey hull and ice-cake superstructure tinged with the flame of the deepening sun, 'Baltic Enterprise' must have presented a formidable sight.

Perhaps some would see her as a snorting, lumbering, burdened workhorse, though anxious to be reunited with her own element after a twelve-hour rest, reluctant to be penned through a narrow corral before being released. Certainly there were noisies to back up such a vision.

First, as her Captain thrust her bow a foot or so one way and then braked the move with a dash of adverse power, they would hear intermittent bursts of clanging vibrations from the head of the oncoming beast. Then as the main bulk advanced there would be the incessant roar of breathing from the fresh-air ventilators sited midway along the accommodation tower. Further, and foremost, as her Master cracked the whip on the main engines to check the eager animal's drift to port, growls of contempt would echo from the sky-high funnel top. Augmenting these volleys of pulsating sound from that elevated voice-box was a perpetual low thud transmitted from the very heart and lifeblood of the brute — its generators.

In reality they did see a 4,667 gross ton ro-ro ship bedecked with steel containers coaxed expertly into the lock-pit. Her smooth progress had been only fractionally impaired. Having virtually turned on a central axis before heading towards the small congregation, the ship had agitated a huge volume of dock water in an anti-clockwise manner. With her bows through the inner gates this backwash swirled below her starboard quarter. Anticipating this involuntary sidestep, Gerry Brazendale had been quick in countering with a brisk four ahead starboard engine, seven astern port. At this the spectators saw the ship gain a positive level glide with the lock walls. On and on until, fully engulfed within the pit, her forward way was finally halted.

Twenty five minutes had elapsed from leaving the ro-ro berth to the shorehands catching the heaving lines thrown by the deck crews and hauling the weighty mooring warps over the white topped bollards at the lockside. Having barely an hour left to run, the flood tide had reduced the drop to the river to eight feet. Anyone who walked to the lock-head at the riverside would see a ten-minute cascade of boiling turbulence as this differential of water was released through the submerged sluices.

Those who stood back purely to view the mass that had arrived and was descending before them would notice it was far from devoid of human habitation. There were men busying themselves with winches both fore and aft. Six passengers were leaning on the rails of the boat deck. Above were three uniformed figures in conference on the overhanging bridge wing. A seventh passenger who had been standing with them was now on the highest part of the superstructure scanning the environs of the Humber through binoculars.

Five miles along the road from my home is one of the most well-known landmarks on the East Coast of England — namely Flamborough Head. Crowning the tip of this scenic promontory, warning off coastal shipping, is a splendidly proportioned lighthouse. Through the summer season Trinity House opens its doors for guided tours of inspection. Hundreds of holidaymakers climb the 119 steps that spiral round the inside of the tapering tower.

It is hardly surprising that being 90 feet above the ground and 240 feet over the sea, the panorama from the lantern room gives coastal views unsurpassed for many miles. Yet if this building were sited alongside the lock at Queen Elizabeth Dock that day it would have barely provided a finer view than that offered from the topmost deck of 'Baltic Enterprise.'

Not that I expected to find a tropical islet inhabited by a family of gibbons above the bridgehouse when it was suggested that the 'monkey island' was the ultimate vantage point aboard ship. But on an evening comparable to those in equatorial latitudes I did expect to find someone taking the evening air from that high promenade. Superseded in height by only the buff painted steel mast and the black band at the funnel-top, the 'monkey island' was the uppermost tier of the ship's superstructure. Flanked by waist high rail-topped coamings its broad green acreage was uninhabited save for a number of strategically placed navigational aids. On deep-sea voyaging this outpost would be used for taking sightings from celestial bodies but on that occasion the vantage was an almost unrestricted 360 degrees vista of Humberside.

By this time the ship was being slowly, ever so slowly, lowered to the river level. Astern countless common gulls darted to and fro before eventually settling on the rippled lake of dock water which, from that high platfom, spread out like a shimmering carpet. Beyond, the skyline revealed the outer fringes of East Hull with its stretches of flat open country dotted here and there with high rise flats and industrial complexes. West-wards, partially silhouetted by falling sunlight, the starboard side faced an urban backcloth which was the heart of the city. Standing out over the roof-tops was the slender wafer building of the Royal Infirmary whilst beyond the redundant cranes at Alexandra Dock the tower of the 13th century Holy Trinity Church was a feature of the riverside. The church is in the Old Town where other buildings prominent in Hull's history are in abundance — The Guildhall, Trinity House, Wilberforce House and the Old Corn Exchange to name but a few. Not the least of

Superstructure from the after deck.

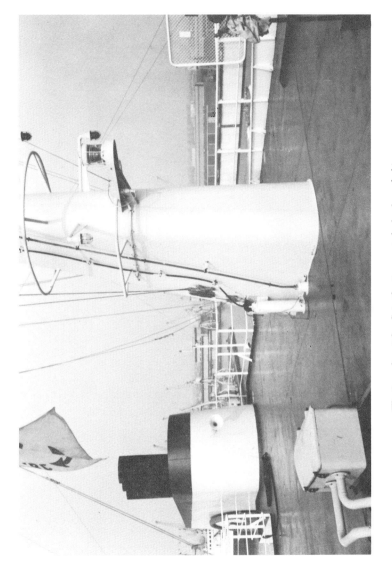

The 'monkey island' is the topmost deck aboard ship.

29

the many curiosities there is a lane named 'Land of Green Ginger.'
Then there was the great river highway in a summertime disguise of
shimmering silver. Being two miles wide at that point the Humber had
gathered great strength. Even on that comparatively quiet evening its
scurrying current tossed and bounced a small cabin cruiser that optimis-
tically punched the last of the tide presumably attempting to reach its
destination before dark.

A glance at a map of Northern England reveals how this river gains its
power. Streams awakening in far-off limestone fells, distant heather-clad
moors and populated valleys hasten on a crooked course to fill a network
of deep rivers on the broad agricultural plains. This estimated 5,000-mile
river system, which drains one fifth of the country, is often described by
taking the Humber as a right forearm with a hand containing some nine
fingers. These tributaries, having a bold assortment of intriguing names —
Swale, Ure, Nidd and Wharfe, Aire, Calder, Don, Derwent and Rye, flow
together to form the palm — the River Ouse. Gaining even further
prosperity from the Rivers Trent and Hull, the Humber surges from the
wrist onwards to the sea, claiming the distinction of being Britain's biggest
watershed.

Upstream, through the glasses, I could see the Humber's crowning
glory. Eight miles distant from the ship's side linking North and South
Banks was the magnificent sweep of the Humber Bridge. With a distance of
4,626 feet between its 525 feet high concrete towers, this masterpiece of civil
engineering boasts the world's longest single span. Eleven thousand tons of
steel wire form the cables that support the $1\frac{1}{4}$-mile roadway beneath.

Still upstream but five miles nearer than the bridge, the South Bank
revealed the New Holland Pier. Before the days of the bridge, this was the
South Bank terminal for the Humber Ferries. These distinctive paddle
steamers plied across from the Corporation Pier on Hull's central
waterfront. Of the paddlers used for many decades on the service, only one
remains on Humberside, that being the 'Lincoln Castle,' which has been
given a new lease of life as a shoreside restaurant a short distance
downstream from the bridge.

Walking over to the port side rail our height advantage over the near
transit sheds allowed a clear view of the Saltend Jetties where two small
rust-streaked tankers were berthed for the purpose of discharging to the
nearby B.P. refinery. Again, accentuated by the low-lying land that
broached its shores, the main impact here was the ever-widening River
Humber. I began to consider the voyage and remembered that on this
occasion the familiar stretch of water before me was the prelude to the
North Sea, the Kattegat, the Baltic and in three days time the Gulf of
Finland.

CHAPTER THREE

Staring at the innumerable Humberside features offered by my new-found vantage, I suddenly became aware of motion. Beyond the neat lines of deck cargo, the squat steel foremast and the curvature of the white bulwarks, the way had been opened to the river. Though I had failed to notice the outer lock gates fold parallel with the gaunt masonry of the pit, I could not detract from the strong blast from the ship's siren as we crept towards the bold Humber fairway. Below me the two Master mariners continued to direct operations from the starbord bridge wing — Brazendale still handling the engine controls — Ashby scanning the river from over the forward protective coamings.

The encounters between Masters and Pilots are brief. There is seldom any social connection to divert their conversation away from the job in hand. They meet purely on business and, since the Pilot normally boards the ship within minutes of the scheduled departure time, any social prelude is generally limited to a hand shake over the Captain's office desk prior to going to the bridge. Replacing the lack of personal friendship is a secure professional etiquette that each strives to respect. In doing so they unite a wealth of nautical expertise to guide a ship safely across uncertain waters. On this occasion, Brazendale, edging the grey and white bulk out of the lock, was the authority over the capricious inclinations of a tightly reined ro-ro ship — Ashby, watching the tide chase by a river buoy, the delegated power over the fickle whims of the Humber.

Down on the extremity of the lock pier the Dock Master, a formidable white-capped figure, transfixed his eyes on the moving steel walls. When finally the stern doors came clearly into his view he issued the all-clear by means of a long shrill note from his pocket whistle.

Now free of the dock confines, the ship was in a position to be brought into a tight port turn of some 100 degrees against the tide onto a seaward heading.

"Hard to port!" Brazendale rasped from the wing.

"Hard to port," echoed back from the shaded interior.

In this situation the effect of the bow thruster was most apparent. With little forward way the rudder position is more or less formality. Here a conventional general cargo freighter would rely heavily on a leading tug to bring her head round into the tideway. But with bow propeller thrusting at full power to starboard, starboard engine at seven ahead and port engine pulled back to six astern, 'Enterprise' reacted with a show of independence. Heeling a degree or two to starboard as her bow scoured the distant Lincolnshire shore, she made short work of finding the direction of the salt air.

"Midships!" During the turn Brazendale had shifted the control position to the bridgehouse. Now it was no longer necessary to bellow the orders; his voice, though quiet, revealed a sharp edge.

"Midships," retorted the man at the wheel.

Standing at the main engine control fascia the Captain turned to Ashby.

31

"Rudder midships and making seven knots, Pilot."

He had set the ship on the broad river fairway bows headed towards the sea and making more than ample steerageway. Obviously this was the signal for Ashby to take over.

John Ashby was a man of cheery disposition. He took command with a bounce of self-confidence.

"Thank you, Captain; one-three-five please."

"One-three-five, steady."

Leaning forward with arms spread against the shining consoles, the Pilot carefully matched 'Enterprise's' idle progress to the dial reading before him. The seven knots recorded there was, of course, the speed we were travelling through the water and not relative to the land. With the last of the tide still producing a two-knot current against us the nearby shore seemed to linger abeam.

"I think we can make that ten knots, Captain."

Gerry Brazendale immediately agreed and hastened to make the necessary adjustments to the neat levers on the dias.

The reason for the gentle pace that the Pilot maintained along those early stretches of deep-water channel known as Hull Roads was to avoid making excessive wash. If she should be opened up to her normal service speed in such close proximity to the shore, a ship with the displacement of 'Baltic Enterprise' would send considerable waves lashing against the river banks, installations or any unfortunate moored craft.

Passing the two protruding jetties at Saltend, where the two well-used coastal tankers laid quietly alongside, we overlooked a landscape shrouded in pipes and storage tanks. Much of the area used to create that chemical refinery, with its inevitable metallic forest, had been born through a land reclamation scheme spanning back many years. It seemed to almost stretch to the town of Hedon two miles away. In medieval times Hedon used to be a port of great importance. But unfortunately the Humber began to silt and eventually cut off the town from the sea. It was due to this fall of fortune that Hull took over as the major port. Contrasting nobly with the foreground B.P. development was the 128 foot tower of the parish church of St. Augustine, which soared high above a tight cluster of pantile roofs.

Out on the port wing, away from an atmosphere marked with dextrous control, the pace was more definable. 'Baltic Enterprise' was beginning to collect herself, pushing dark wedges of murky water scornfully away from her towering sides. The Pilot was steering us along the deep-water channel that initially clung to the north bank. The steady forward motion had turned the evening air decidedly cooler and with every yard we travelled one could anticipate the awaiting tang of the sea. In this sedate attitude 'Enterprise' seemed to have regained a certain dignity that every ship loses when bound to the quay of harbour or dock. This aloof contentment could be detected through the audible change in her attendant noises drifting over the stern. It could be felt in the gentle vibrations through her rails. It could be seen as the black soot-filled exhaust gave way to a blurr of hot grey air from the funnel top.

Once away from port, the normal shipboard routine of watch-keeping settles down. In this respect a roll-on roll-off vessel conforms to the practice common to all British registered merchant ships. Besides the Master, who under normal circumstances does not stand watch, 'Baltic Enterprise' carried the accepted minimum of three watchkeeping navigating officers. Likewise, the engineering section was made up of three watchkeeping officers who were directly responsible to the Chief Engineer. These six men stood watches of one four-hour period in every twelve. Consequently each man had two spells of duty every day spent at sea in this rotation:

	Bridge	Engine Room
00.01 — 04.00	Second Officer	Third Engineer
04.00 — 08.00	Chief Officer	Second Engineer
08.00 — 12.00	Third Officer	Fourth Engineer
12.00 — 16.00	Second Officer	Third Engineer
16.00 — 20.00	Chief Officer	Second Engineer
20.00 — 00.01	Third Officer	Fourth Engineer

Completing the ship's complement of eleven officers were three additional non-watchkeepers — the Electrical Officer, who was attached to the engineering section — the Radio Officer, who had fixed hours of manning by day and, being accommodated adjacent to the radio room, was on twenty-four-hour standby — and, of course, the Catering Officer, whose busy daytime routine I had already sampled.

Other ranks of registered seamen, greasers, cooks and stewards made up the ship's total crew number to twenty-six men.

As we trod a path past the Anson and Hebble buoys, I was joined at the rail by Peter Green. He had just been relieved from watch by Third Officer Willie Maclaughlan. Being now 20.30 hours I commented on the late change-over. Here Green explained that when entering or leaving port, regardless of what time of day, all navigating, or deck officers as they are often called, are on duty. On 'Baltic Enterprise' it was practice for the Chief Officer to be on the bridge with the Captain. The Second Officer took charge of the after mooring deck and operated the stern door mechanism while the Third Officer supervised the forward mooring deck. Our departure time had more or less coincided with Green's watch. Now off duty he was looking forward to a relaxing hour in the Officers' Smoke Room before turning in for an early night.

With two miles of the Humber behind and twenty ahead, we watched the tiny riverside village of Paull slip quietly by. Though the distance between ship and shore was steadily widening, the squat white tower of the lighthouse at the waterfront looked only a stone's throw away. It has stood there since 1836 when the Brethren of Trinity House deemed the necessity of a navigational light on that stretch of shore. It is no longer used for that purpose however, for it was sold and ultimately converted into a unique private residence commanding unrivalled views of river traffic. But a few hundred yards downstream of Paull we passed a small shipyard.

Surprisingly in the days of decline in both fishing and shipbuilding industries, it was kept busy constructing middle distance trawlers.

A sudden change of exhaust tempo announced that more had been called of the engines. They struck up in unison to promote a bold harmonious thunder that gripped the after decks. A distinct pulse from underfoot augmented this business-like proclamation. As Peter Green and I ambled aft along the wide steel deck the effect of the increased power was more than evident. 'Enterprise' had awakened from her muted stride to produce a deep traumatic influence on the Humber tideway. A succession of white-topped curling waves splayed with great fervour from her sheer sides. Twenty feet below the surface, the thrashing propellers ejected a watery meringue that spread a wake twice the width of the ship.

"That will be ten ahead both engines — probably seventeen knots," Peter Green informed me above the exhaust noise.

He was to add however that until we were out on the open sea the engines were normally governed back to 80% of full power. Despite the application of 'full ahead' we were still running just short of usual service speed.

"Once clear of the Humber we ask the engine room for 90% power. This will give us something like eighteen to nineteen knots."

With Hull slowly disappearing from view, we reflected that the weekend was just beginning. Factories and offices would have closed their doors until Monday morning. Friday night revellers would be turning out to the pubs, discos, clubs, cinemas and inevitable bingo halls. People starting annual holidays would be in the act of loading their cars in readiness for an early morning assault on Britain's motorways. The docks, now we had taken our leave, would be enveloped in the quiet of a promised tranquility.

Truly, the setting from the aft rail was unreal. Almost at its full height the tide had swallowed the mud banks and saltings that are all too familiar to those who frequent that unpredictable waterway. Disguised in the glow of a low fiery sun the murky expanse of the Humber and its dull shores took on a semblance of some exotic riviera.

While we marvelled at that rare scene, Bo'sun Peter Edwards appeared on the deck below. He unceremoniously lowered the Red Ensign that throughout the day had been fluttering at a tall staff that angled aft from the rails beneath us. All British ships display flags known as the Red, White, and Blue Ensigns respectively. They originated when the British fleet was divided into three squadrons, each squadron being represented by a colour — red then being senior. In 1864 these colour squadrons were abolished. Directions were then issued, which are still in force, that the White Ensign should be used by men-of-war, the Blue Ensign by vessels of the Royal Naval Reserve and the Red Ensign by merchantmen and vessels of fishing fleets. There is a clause whereby a merchant vessel may fly the Blue Ensign when the Master or a certain number of the officers and ratings are Royal Naval reservists.

The large flag that Edwards carefully folded is normally flown while the ship is in port. At sea a smaller version of this flag was flown together with the house flag from the mainmast from sunrise to sunset.

Among a host of duties for which he is directly responsible to the Chief Officer, the Bo'sun and his men spend much of the daytime painting the upper structure of the ship. Seizing the opportunity of a quick progress report from his subordinate, Green quietly excused himself and was away down the steel stairway.

Ten miles out of Hull the deep-water channel closed in on the South Bank. There an unpopulated marshy shoreline had given way to a vast complex of industrial development. First, extending from that arena, were the Killingholme Oil Terminal jetties. Here our Pilot brightly asked for a reduction in speed. Brazendale, hovering around the starboard side of the bridgehouse anticipating the request, brought both engine controls backwards until the five ahead reading was displayed. Simultaneously a prolonged accompaniment of released air pressure hissed from beneath the console. This was a sound not unlike that issued from the brakes of a commercial vehicle, but less characteristic was the rate of deceleration; it was barely detectable.

Between calling for course alterations first five degrees one way and then the other, Ashby talked about pilotage of supertankers on the Humber. It was alongside these South Bank jetties that the true giants of the ocean discharge crude oil from the Arabian Gulf. Seemingly the larger vessels of this class arrive after discharging half their cargoes at Rotterdam. In this state they can be drawing between forty and fifty feet of water and moor at Immingham less than a mile downstream from Killingholme. Until recently it had been practice for the Pilot to join such a vessel ten miles out from the coast. This, in bad weather, is a long and sometimes hazardous trip for the small Pilot launches. After such a passage to the rendezvous point, a Pilot could be feeling somewhat under par — indeed not a situation one would wish to be in when about to commence the close navigation of a huge ship. However it has become a regular practice for the Pilot to be sent to Rotterdam via North Sea Ferries to join the supertanker. After enjoying the voyage to Holland as a passsanger he would then return in the same capacity on the oil tanker before commencing duties at the ten-mile approach to the Humber.

It would seem that this is an amicable arrangement for both Pilot and ship's Master alike. Initially it can take several miles and up to twenty-five minutes in time to slow a 250,000 dwt. tanker from its normal service speed of sixteen knots to a suitable pick-up speed. When eventually bought to a near halt they soon begin to loose steerageway and, even in a gentle wind, will quickly start to sheer off course. Hence the distinct advantage for the Master knowing that having the Pilot already aboard he has not to stop his ship in a strange, crowded and relatively shallow seaway.

Apart from the physical problems that evolve through such a manoeuvre the time factor can also be a crucial element. Like ro-ro ships, and sometimes even more so, supertankers are subject to stringent timetables. Dire efforts are regularly made by their Masters to adhere to them. This has been highlighted through unfortunate disasters that have occurred where in cutting a corner to save a few miles and precious minutes tanker Masters have put their ships on the rocks. Each stage of a tanker's turn-round is scrupulously programmed. Even the half-hour taken in stopping, engaging the Pilot and getting underway again could mean missing a tide in a few weeks time in some place at the other side of the world .

Asbhy was a man who had guided and steered ships on the fickle Humber from a bridge set a quarter mile from the bows. "Every manoeuvre has to be planned much earlier than those on an average ship — supertankers do not respond to quick decisions! When aboard one feels isolated from the water. Mainly this is brought about through the bridge being one hundred feet or more above the surface and having to walk nearly twice that distance from one side to see what is happening at the other. Fortunately maritime regulations covering 'Rules of the road' have recently been extensively revised to give supertankers the right of way in restricted waters. To claim this priority they have to show certain lights and give advance warning of their approach." Disappointingly on that Friday evening the tanker berths at both Killingholme and Immingham stood empty and unattended. There was however much else on that South Bank to catch the eye. Hereabouts, while holding ten knots, we passed the entrance to Immingham Dock. This is the Humber's busiest port. It is claimed that in the mid-70's Immingham was handling a volume of cargo exceeding that of both Hull and Liverpool combined. Whereas Hull gained impetus as a port during the 17th, 18th and 19th centuries, Immingham owes its fame to more recent times, this being attributed to the development of the huge steelworks at Scunthorpe in the early 20th century.

The bridge of our ship was sufficiently elevated to afford a useful view. Certainly the metropolis of deep-sea ships, oil storage units, cranes, sheds and office blocks would contrive a scene far removed from the Immingham Creek that the Pilgrim Fathers knew in 1608. It was from there that they originally set sail before crossing the Atlantic in 1620. Street names at the nearby village of South Killingholme commemorate that occasion.

While gazing across at Immingham my thoughts sprang back to another original voyage from there, the occasion being a memorable first-time sea voyage to the continent for my wife and I. The opportunity arose when in 1967 the Swedish Tor Line Company opened up new sea links between Gothenburg, Immingham and Amsterdam for a sparkling new 7,000 gross ton car, cargo, passenger ferry 'Tor Anglia.' Part of Tor Line's inauguration programme was the operation of wintertime mini-cruises between Immingham and Amsterdam departing Friday evenings to return the following Sunday morning. I well remember after a week of doubtful speculation over the voyage the ninety-mile drive from Bridlington one freezing cold February night — also the pleasant surprise we received when on arrival with one hour to spare for the 10 p.m. scheduled departure we caught sight of 'Tor Anglia' resplendantly floodlit from stem to stern against a starry sky. Further to our approval was the warm Scandinavian hospitality shown both at the brand-new terminal building and on embarking into the ship's sumptuous interior.

We were trail-blazing on a new service and in this respect our dubious

36

approach had been fuelled by our travel agent having very limited information, but even more so by the ridiculously low cost of the trip. At only £8 per head the cruise included return fare to Amsterdam, two nights dinner, bed and breakfast en route with accommodation in a two-berth cabin, a two-hour guided coach tour of Amsterdam followed by lunch in a city centre hotel. As an added stimulus to the voyage caviar was included on the 'smorgasbord' for the return crossing. Today the fare sounds unbelievable but even in the late 60's it represented incredible value for money.

Throughout the following years Tor Line have built up a considerable fleet of ro-ro ships. After the heading of 'Tor,' each bears a name representative of a North European country or ancient territory. Though Tor Line operate an extensive freight business out of Immingham they abandoned passenger services from the port during the mid 70's. Eventually 'Tor Anglia' and her sister 'Tor Hollandia' were replaced by the spectacular 15,000 gross ton 'Tor Britannia' and 'Tor Scandinavia.' These blue and white super ferries operate on regular services between Felixstowe, Gothenburg and Amsterdam. Latterly, 'Tor Scandinavia' has been star of the television serial 'Triangle.'

With Immingham astern, 'Baltic Enterprise' continued seaward along the broad lane of buoys and marks that she had obediently followed from her berth. Because the river current is often running fast and strong many of the Humber marks are set on double-ended steel boats, flush decked and giving every appearance of scaled-down lightships. Under such conditions some conventional buoys become deceptive, primarily through straining at the limit of their moorings and adopting a horizontal attitude.

Occasionally the Pilot would point out buoys and marks; some were named after the sands they guard — Clay Huts, Holm Hook, Burcom and Clee Ness — others had just been re-sited because of ever-shifting sand and mud banks.

"The Humber charts require constant updating to accommodate these changes," Ashby said.

Although regulations demand that a Pilot should be engaged to navigate ships upwards of 1,500 tons on such waters, it is the Master who shoulders ultimate responsibility should anything go wrong. If a Master suspects that his ship is being steered into danger he is at liberty to over-ride the pilot's instructions. Though this occurrence is not commonplace I have heard of ship's Masters who have disagreed with the specialist navigator, more often than not when in foreign water. Generally language difficulties bring the situation to fruit. This break-down of communication usually leads to a misunderstanding of the ship's handling performance or a misinterpretation of a command.

The probability of such happenings aboard 'Enterprise' that evening seemed as remote as the stars that were beginning to peep through the darkening backcloth. Though temporarily dispossessed of his command, Brazendale seemed totally relaxed, showing no indication of questioning the Pilot's judgement. Clearly contributing to this self-assurance was the way in which Ashby not only gave intelligible decisive orders but offered a cheerful explanation for his actions to those who happened to be within earshot. When driving a car one has to think in terms of half a mile ahead and a few hundred yards behind — when navigating a heavily laden ro-ro ship on the brisk Humber tideway one has to think in a range of ten times that distance; Ashby was doing just that.

The Spurn Pilot Station from which the 150 registered Humber Pilots operate has been labelled as the most modern of its kind around Britain's shores. Prior to its opening in 1976 duty Pilots were based aboard the old Pilot cutter 'William Fenton,' which was moored in the lee of Spurn headland. Sometimes, due to spells of bad weather, the inadequacy of that arrangement led to temporary closure of the service. The new shore station provided the Pilot with sophisticated radar and communications systems. It operates at a much higher degree of efficiency and at a fraction of the cost of building a new cutter to present-day standards. It is manned throughout the twenty-four hours by a Pilot Master, an assistant Pilot and a clerk. In bad weather the Pilot Master can call any other Pilots on duty roster to provide back-up assistance on radar surveillance. This means that unlike many stations in Britain and Europe it is manned only to requirement and not continually to peak traffic density. Alongside the control centre there is a pier that extends 850 feet out into the Humber. This provides for a minimum depth of nine feet of water; therefore, the Pilot launches are fully operational at all states of the tide.

The upper floor of the six-tier building is the second part of the Spurn 'uplift.' Utilising the vantage gained from that level are the Humber District Coastguards who also maintain a round-the-clock vigil over the estuary.

It is said that over the centuries, Spurn Peninsula has gradually risen from the sea through millions of tons of eroded sand, gravel and boulder clay being swept down the Yorkshire Coast. On meeting the fierce Humber cross-current this wasted land matter has been thrown up to form a three-mile finger-like ridge where little grows except coarse marram grass and a selection of wild flowers. In many places this narrow tract of land is no wider than the bumpy road that runs along its entire length. The road not only provides a landline for the Pilots and coastguards but is the principal link with civilisation for the small community of permanent residents at the 'Point.'

The neat row of simple cottages that nestles amid the dunes at Spurn are the homes of the Humber lifeboatmen and their families. Due to its remoteness and demands called upon it, the Humber Lifeboat has the distinction of being the only R.N.L.I. craft to be manned by a full-time crew. Being a high-pressure station covering a sometimes menacing seaway crowded with ships running for shelter, the Institution deemed to post one of their most up-to-date vessels at Spurn. Only a hundred yards of sandy track separate the cottages from the jetty near which 'City of Bradford IV' awaits permanently in the water. She is an 'Arun' class lifeboat, a design that was developed through years of stringent trials in all conceivable conditions. Incorporating every feasible ounce of technical know-how in her 54 foot hull, she powers along at 18 knots — almost double the speed of the majority of offshore lifeboats. There is a choice of two control positions and should it be necessary up to 30 rescued people can be accommodated in the warmth of her fully enclosed cabin.

In common with all R.N.L.I. stations, Spurn has a long history of brave men who have fearlessly challenged the dangers of the sea. Though one could devote an entire volume to these heroes, I make no excuses for mentioning within these pages the recent achievement of these men in a sequence of courageous rescues; events that led to the present Coxswain of the Humber Lifeboat, Brian Bevan, being the first man in 155 years of lifeboat history to be awarded Gold, Silver and Bronze gallantry medals at one time.

During the night of February 14th, 1979, both the Humber men and the 'Arun' boat were put to the ultimate test when they put to sea on what was described as one of the most hazardous missions ever attempted by the Humber Lifeboat. In the height of a freezing winter storm, the Panamanian registered coaster 'Revi,' thirty miles north-east off the Humber bound for Newcastle from Port Longuet, France, sent out a 'mayday' after her cargo of silver sand had shifted. Her tarpaulin covers had ripped and in the big seas she took on water fast — soon developing a forty-five degree list. Battering her way to the 'Revi' the lifeboat encountered such seas that her crew of eight had to lash themselves to the deck for safety. On arrival at the scene Coxswasin Bevan mounted a daring operation lasting forty-five minutes during which the lifeboat made no fewer than thirty-five run-and-snatch attempts before the last of the 'Revi's' four-man crew was rescued.

Sometimes the stern of the coaster was raised twenty-five feet in the air above the lifeboat leaving Bevan desperately trying to judge his run-in for when the two vessels would be on equal terms. One of the most hazardous moments of the night occurred when 'City of Bradford' went in to rescue the German Captain of the 'Revi' — the last man left on board. The coaster suddenly rose up on a gigantic wave and threatened to crash down on the lifeboat. Bevan managed to avoid disaster by inches but the captain seemed to disappear. By then the waves were washing completely over the coaster and Bevan realised he would have to run in yet again regardless. Exactly five minutes after the captain had finally leapt to safety the 'Revi' keeled over and sank.

The official report made by the R.N.L.I. on the rescue states: "The courage, seamanship and expertise required to carry out this remarkable night service in appalling storm conditions, combined with snow and ice-cold water constantly breaking over the crew, necessitating about thirty-five separate occasions of going alongside, was absolutely outstanding and in the best traditions of the R.N.L.I."

It goes on: "In addition the leadership and initiative shown by Coxswain Bevan was of the highest order and was clearly demonstrated by the confidence his crew showed in him whilst they were in such great danger themselves on the foredeck, with their lives completely in his hands throughout the rescue."

At the age of thirty-two, Brian Bevan was awarded the R.N.L.I. Gold Medal; each of his crewmen received the Bronze Medal. Within a short period of that winter, Bevan had notched up two more rescues of similar daring meriting the Silver and Bronze Medals. He and his crew received their awards from the Duke of Kent at the Royal Festival Hall, London. In their absence a full standby crew was posted at the Spurn Station.

It was the beam of Spurn Lighthouse piercing the dusk that gave the initial visual bearing of the headland. But shortly, with 'Enterprise' scything away the remaining ten river miles, Spurn Peninsula rose from the horizon in the guise of a low undulating breakwater. To starboard the lofty 1,000,000 brick hydraulic tower on the Grimsby waterfront had been the last significant landmark; from there on the Lincolnshire shoreline had filtered into obscurity. To all appearances we were on an open seaway confronted only by a finger of land that reached down from an indefinable north shore. In the bridgehouse the shirt-sleeved Maclaughlan, unprompted by his superior, removed the daylight masks from the three radar consoles, the faces of the Captain and Pilot then being warmed intermittently by a rich orange glow as, in turn, they wandered to and from the informative screens.

The 128 foot tower of the Spurn light which was providing the only landmark of any substance stands somewhere in the vicinity of what is claimed to be Britain's very first lighthouse. As early as 1428 a hermit, Richard Reedbarrow, devoted himself to erecting a tower to warn off shipping from the headland. From his hermitage at the village of Ravenspurne, Reedbarrow had watched a succession of ships wrecked on the shifting sands with the loss of countless lives and tons of cargo. Ironically, his tower, that served as a beacon by day and a light by night, together with his home, was washed away by the sea shortly after he had secured the right to impose a levy on the tonnage that passed safely by.

During the following years several towers were built and then purposely demolished when it was found the sands had shifted and the beacon had become deceptive. Later John Smeaton, builder of the Eddystone Lighthouse, built two consecutive towers at Spurn but neither survived the storms that periodically ravish the headland. Eventually Ravenspurne itself joined the long line of east coast villages that have been devoured by the sea. Though modernisation has made it an unmanned light, today's Spurn Lighthouse stands much as it was built in 1895.

090 — 085 — 095 — 105 were the commands given by John Ashby to guide the ship along a thread of twinkling navigation marks during the final miles of the river journey. He was busier now, not the least in raising contact with the Pilot launch which was to rendezvous with 'Enterprise' to effect his departure. The launch, which surprisingly was blessed with my surname, 'Mitchell,' was engaged with stablemate 'Fox' shifting Pilots to and from a flotilla of ships riding at anchor around the river mouth.

For the earlier stages of the river passage we had encountered only the odd coastal freighter making either for the wharfs of the River Trent or the 'inland' port of Goole that lies fifty miles upstream from the sea. But the latter stages of the broad waterway became increasingly busy with a wide variety of merchant tonnage — coasters, tankers, a 40,000 dwt. ore carrier 'Appleby,' conventional freighters and ro-ro's in plenty. An inference of the ro-ro image within today's shipping industry was spelled out clearly by the words FAST LINE emblazoned along the hull of an inbound cargo ferry. A closer inspection as she passed by our port side revealed her name as 'Fast One.'

"Cargo only, Rotterdam — Hull," Ashby called over as he saw me resort to binoculars.

These days owners see the towering sides of their ships as free advertising space, ro-ro's and passenger ferries providing an obvious hoarding. To date U.B.C. ships are among the minority of short-sea traders that have been spared that indignity though I suspect, in all probability, none of the fleet is sufficient in length to bear the company's full title in letters of any size.

Soon we closed in on Spurn. Half a mile abeam of the port rail the ghost-like formation of the headland was spearheaded with the pilot station itself. This was a structure not unlike the control tower of a small airport. From its darkened windows the Pilot Master and Coastguard would be observing the solid form of our ship as we glided smartly by. Behind the pilot station the tall black and white banded lighthouse spread its warning at regular ten-second intervals over river and sea. Over and beyond the buildings at the 'Point' the eerie form of Spurn Headland disappeared into a watery background.

The entire spectrum of that strange place induced the imagination to seeing it as a massive deeply-laden supership sailing towards the night. Beyond its great rounded bow was a bridgehouse flanked by flickering lights of accommodation areas. Abaft was a tall mast beaming out a warning to those who should venture into its path. Its hull was represented by the long reaching finger of sand that spread endlessly into the dusk.

Eventually a message from the Pilot launch crackled over the console-mounted loudspeaker.

"Mitchell to Baltic Enterprise, do you read me?"

"Baltic Enterprise — Mitchell — affirmative."

"Can make it in ten minutes, that okay?"

Ashby hesitated, momentarily scanned the sea-lane ahead, then announced:

"Sounds okay to me, see you in ten minutes — out."

At Spurn Lightship, four miles out from the headland, Brazendale assumed full command of his ship. Following a last-minute consultation and firm handshake with Ashby, he immediately asserted his authority across the bridgehouse to both men remaining there.

"Starboard five!"

Then turning to Maclaughlan in a quiet tone asked:

"Will you escort the Pilot to the deck, please?"

From the starboard wing I watched a high-speed launch race out of the gloom. Our ship was now at a subdued "three ahead," welcoming the Pilot craft alongside.

41

Of strong business-like lines, these launches were built to the design of the Arun lifeboat. In the half light she swept almost past only to whisk into a tight 150 degrree starboard turn. 'Mitchell' heeled and bounced on the fickle water that had been aroused by the slowing ship. Dwarfed by 'Enterprise's high-rise sides she was soon tucked in close and obscured from view to all except those who overhung the outer rails.

Maclaughlan and the departing Pilot were at a hatchway on the starboard side of the weather deck. From there a steel ladder led through the innards to the lower tween deck where a small Pilot door had been opened. The last lap of the descent to the sea was by means of a short rope ladder that dangled vertically from this door over the ship's side.

Pacing continually between the bridgehouse and starboard wing, Brazendale was intent on retarding his ship's pace to effect a smooth pick-up yet holding sufficient steerage way.

"Starboard ten!"

The burly helmsman, who in strong voice had promptly repeated the calls from both Master and Pilot on our river passage, had been stood down to an older man whose narrow face was brought from the shadows by the gentle illumination of the compass rose.

"I called Starboard ten, could you speak up please?"

Brazendale, through the gentle swing of the bow, had detected the application of his order but not heard the customary response. His caustic tones of admonishment received an immediate reply.

"Starboard ten, Captain."

"Steady as she goes!" Brazendale bellowed.

"Steady as she goes." Though troubled with a croaky voice, the new helmsman was more than anxious to reply.

John Ashby had wasted no time in descending to the launch. Clutching his small document case in one hand the Pilot laconically turned a glance skywards and waved into the big ship's searchlight with the other. Brazendale reciprocated in similar vein as he watched the gap between the two vessels widen. For a time the bridgehouse atmosphere was much the poorer for the absence of Ashby. His lively banter and knowledgeable commentary were past. Rightly Brazendale and his third officer were fully involved in the business of clearing the coast and heading the ship towards Scandinavia.

Now that his presence was more meaningful the keen-eyed young Scotsman worked at the Master's right hand fulfilling various mandatory functions. The correct charts had to be available at a second's notice while at the same table the ship's log had to be kept up to date.

"Full away at 21.51," Brazendale had called in the direction of the illuminated table.

Then the internal telephone buzzed with calls, resulting in two seamen walking out to the bow to 'secure anchors' and the duty engineer, Paul Davey, opening the main engine governors to allow 90% of maximum power.

Brazendale switched 'Enterprise' onto automatic pilot and promptly

42

dismissed the seaman from the wheel. To starboard only the lights of approximately twenty ships either at anchor or gingerly making their approach to the river mouth separated us from the wide ocean. The redundant helmsman was posted to the wing to keep watchful eye over them.

During the hours of darkness it is practice for these ships to carry a 'look-out' on the bridge. To be more exact the on-duty seaman is stationed on the wings to give observational assistance to the navigation officer.

Maclaughlan joined the seaman at the starbord rail. With an outstretched arm he scoured the blackened horizon indicating the lights on which he required special watch.

Striking out for the Humber Lightship (ten miles from the coast and the last staging post before the long reach to Northern Denmark) 'Baltic Enterprise' settled on eighteen and a half knots, issuing no more than the gentle ''lolling' motion of a lake steamer. Astern, beyond our silver wake, the shore lights were being drawn away as though on invisible strings becoming smaller and smaller until they were drowned by the inky ocean. One thousand and fifty miles ahead a Helsinki ro-ro berth lay waiting. Above, the exhausts thundered their rhythmic bark into the night sky. Below a cosy bar, a tray of sandwiches and a comfortable bed were signalling a welcome.

Two 5,250 h.p. diesels power the ship along at 18½ knots.
(Foto Flite, Ashford, Kent)

CHAPTER FOUR

My route to work each morning carries me along the sea-front. There are several routes from which to choose to make the journey but my car seems automatically programmed to follow the shoreline.

From the Esplanade, which for seventy per cent of the year is totally deserted at that time of day, I look out at the broad sweep of Bridlington Bay. Each day, regardless of the time of year, I find the picture one of continuous change.

There are days when huge white-topped waves roll in from the south-east finally to expend their energies against age-old stone piers at the harbour in thirty-foot high festoons. These angry seas emit a salt-laden mist that drifts across the town filming windows and dampening the spirits of those who shop in the streets. Should the wind be from the north-west, which in winter is so often, the scene changes completely. Now the seascape is one of ships at anchor. I have counted as many as forty at one time — coasters, tugs, trawlers, coastal tankers; sometimes larger vessels — container ships and conventional freighters alike. They ride there scattered in threes and fours on a blue-grey mass of unsettled water yet retain a reasonable level plane. Looking out across the horzion on such a day one realises the amount of shelter these ships are enjoying for beyond the protective arm of Flamborough Head the familiar horizontal line has contorted into a water roller-coaster. At first glance it would appear to be an optical illusion. On focusing the glasses out there however, one recognises the skyline undulations as waves of thirty feet or more.

For all that I pass within fifty yards of the sea-edge there are times when poor visibility blots out any hope of a peep at the tide-line let alone a prospect of the bay. These heavy sea frets do not come unannounced; the fog signal on the headland attends to that. The mist nearly always seems to blanket the Flamborough promontory before the beaches at Bridlington. When it approaches the fog horn bellows a remorseless double 'moan' every ninety seconds. On hearing the 'ailing cow' broadcasting, I know, even before stepping outdoors, that a vista of the sea is off the cards.

I would not wish to give an impression that life by the North Sea is perpetually shrouded in the grip of bad weather. Many are the mornings when the sun, rising over the horizon, casts an air of 'tropical splendour' around the bay. It opens up a paint-box of colour contrasts that suffuse from a theme of deep blue. Snow-white cliffs topped in a verdant lustre of tree and grass, sea-front hotels kissed with the yellow gold light shimmering off the water and tawny rich sands rim the land as far as the eye can carry. Understandably on such mornings the car seems to linger, reluctant to complete the journey.

At some part of the week I see the local fishing fleet putting to sea. Having left the harbour at intervals of a few minutes they are usually spread out in an easterly direction in line astern. During the summer months the 70 foot keel boats take off for four-day trips. Rigged for off-shore trawling they work up to 120 miles from the coast.

From the open deck of a modern roll-on roll-off cargo freighter bearing 052 degress across the North Sea, I looked out at the horizon. For all it was the same sea, the vista that normally confronted me at this time of day was many horizons distant over our port quarter. The morning was superb and today I had time in plenty to linger.

We had moved on into Saturday in the company of a light westerly breeze and an endless succession of kindly faced waves. The sea had caught the mood of the sky and now two hundred miles of vivid blue water separated 'Baltic Enterprise' from Hull and the River Humber.

On reflection I suppose anyone making for Scandinavia in a much smaller craft may not have looked upon those North Sea corrugations with such an easy mind. But gazing down upon them from the security of the high-riding weather deck one could be excused for taking their worth with total unconcern for, one after another, they submitted to the complete destruction offered by the racing bulk of the ship. As we bore down upon them in progressive slaughter the value of their resistance was smashed, churned and creamed into a bleached fairway of confused water that extended a mile and beyond astern. By way of a respectful gesture in the face of this watery massacre, 'Enterprise' had adopted a gentle side-to-side roll. This, as opposed to the almost terra-firma-like stability we had experienced the previous evening, gave one a not unpleasant feeling of actually being at sea.

Walking out to the bow alongside the lofty lines of containers, I looked

Speeding across the North Sea.

46

Finnish paper loaded on the upper 'tween deck.

on a sea devoid of shipping of any sizeable significance. There were one or two motionless dots that I assumed to be working fishing vessels; that apart, nothing more than sea and sky. Overnight our arrow-like course had carried us to the south of the Dogger Bank. Peter Green had confirmed this when earlier I had dropped in for a surprise post-dawn bridge visit. The Bank is an underwater shelf of sand extending 170 miles from north to south by 60 miles from east to west. The least depth over the Bank is 14 metres. For generations it has proved to be one of the North Sea's most lucrative fishing areas, so it was hardly surprising that we should meet trawlers in the vicinity.

When the weather promises to cut rough the fishing fleets give the 'Bank' a wide berth.

"Big winds and 'short water' means steep seas," a local fisherman once told me.

Green too endorsed that statement by indicating that in severe North Sea conditions the Dogger Bank was avoided even by ships of the likes of 'Enterprise.'

A major landmark in the history of those waters was the 'Dogger Bank Incident' when, in 1904, the Russian Navy attacked a Hull fishing fleet. The Russian battleships and cruisers mistook the fishing vessels for Japanese torpedo boats and inadvertently opened fire. One trawler was sunk, two crewmen killed and several fishing boats badly damaged. The incident brought Britain and Russia to the brink of war. It was only after the Royal Navy put to sea that the Czar apologised for the mistake. The Russian fleet eventually continued on its way — unfortunately for them this lead to annihilation at the hands of the real Japanese in the Far East.

On arrival at the forward mooring deck, I found a three-cornered area enveloped on two sides by ranging solid bulwarks that splayed forward in unison to form the ship's rounded forepeak. Behind was a high wall of steel running athwart ships. This fortress not only formed a barrier between the weather deck cargo and the mooring gear but acted as the foundation of the squat foremast. Hawsers and winches, anchor chains, hawse pipes and windlasses, this was the main furniture up front. Everything tidily secured into place, well greased and carefully painted. This wasn't gear designed only to take strain (which it did in large degrees); it had to take weather also. On such a day it was difficult to envisage huge seas crashing over that high bow, but they did, and all the mechanism there had to survive and function afterwards.

The most striking feature about that lonely outpost was the feeling of detachment from the rest of the ship. This was chiefly brought about through the absence of any mechanical noise or vibration which, though we had been at sea a modest twelve hours, one had subconsciously become adapted to. Not that life within the superstructure was furnished with a perpetual teeth-chattering ausculation of pounding engines and juddering propellers — I would not wish to give that illusion. Yet the steady whisper from the fresh-air ducts in every room together with a definite underfoot shuddering with its attendant noises induced through the transmission of ten thousand five hundred horsepower to the propellers promoted an awarenes of the driving force beneath.

So apparent was the transition from that aliveness to the blunt water-shedding sounds echoing upwards through the hawse pipes that the two places seemed to belong to separate worlds. One indication only of the power being exerted 150 yards abaft was the rolling cascade of seawater anxiously splaying away from the unstoppable grey bow. Standing there, excelling in the morning sunshine and salt-tanged air, I could for all intents have been on some remote headland overlooking a vast blue ocean to the distant tune of the moving tide.

On the aft deck things were different. Behind the accommodation block, the vibrations were strong to the extent of shaking the miscellany of steel fittings into a symphony of metallic crescendos. The broad area of deck was alive with an unseen force. This was a place of work. Again there were huge winches and raised high above the stern rails, blocking any prospect of a rearward view, were the upper ends of the stern doors. The electrical control mechanism of these massive blockades stood across the wide transom in the form of two shoulder high white painted cabinets. A small crane that was used for hoisting stores aboard tremored above the starboard rail.

I wasn't the only person to be out and about at that early hour; there were men swilling the upper decks. This I discovered on narrowly avoiding a drenching from above. Bo'sun Edwards and his deck crew held this long-brush and water cannon event each day. Particularly after leaving port, the exhausts blasted a rime of hot soot skywards. Some of this black grit deposited itself on the apple green decks of the after end. Without regular attention it would have been walked (much to John Garvey's dismay) onto the sacred alleyway carpets.

The "watch out below!" cries that saved me from an unscheduled shower came as I approached an open door in the after bulkhead of the superstructure. Emitting from that door was the exclusive aroma of grilled bacon. In the galley two white-coated cooks moved industriously around a centre island stove. I did not enter to impede this good work — breakfast could not wait!

There have to be times when passengers aboard working ships feel 'left out of things.' Mealtimes are the only programmed gatherings and even as such these occasions do not always attract a high volume of fraternisation from the crew. Not that the officers are intent on being unsociable towards their paying guests — on the contrary, many is the time an off-duty man has yarned long after the table has been cleared and the dishes racked. For the crew mealtimes are the sole occasions when a group of them assemble. As such some may be just going on duty and others ready for bed rest after a heavy four-hour commitment, they may not have the time or inclination to enter into conversation with their fellow officers let alone socialise with strange faces.

These are times when engineers and navigators meet face to face in contrast to their distant telephone communications between engine room and bridge — when 'Sparks' briefly descends from his high mission in the radio room — and when the Catering Officer breaks away from his stock and requisition sheets. During these fleeting get-togethers they talk shop. Whether it's a faulty valve in the engine room, an increase in freight rates or medical course for senior officers, mealtimes provide the opportunity to air their views. These are men in their working environment. They are individual members of a team enrolled to sail the ship safely and on schedule. That is their job, that is what they are paid for, that is what they talk about.

Passengers using the U.K. — Finland services generally fall within three specific groups — business people, holiday travellers and transport drivers. It is doubtful whether any of these people expect or desire to be thrown into an extravaganza of shipboard entertainment by a wily cruise director. If they do expect this they are to be sadly disappointed. Regardless of their comfortable accommodation these are working ships, working under pressure. Hauling thousands of tons of cargo around Northern Europe is their bread and butter; passengers add only the barest covering of jam.

Apart from myself, the ensemble of passengers who, after the 8 a.m. breakfast call, had drifted into the dining saloon that Saturday morning fitted snugly into the three categories. Bob and Ruth Turnbull were to travel alongside me for the round voyage. They had left a thriving Birmingham retail business in the hands of their son and his wife to take two weeks relaxation. They liked the sea but could not stand crowds or regimentation — cruise ships were out. They had been on conventional cargo ships on a number of short sea voyages; this was their first taste of a ro-ro vessel.

Taking the opportunity of mixing a summertime business trip and a short Scandinavian holiday, David Jackson, accompanied by his wife Jean and teenage daughter Susan, would be driving his car off 'Enterprise' at Helsinki on Monday afternoon. In the meantime they were to spend almost three days of waterborne travel in a quiet and relaxed mood. David Jackson had three calls to make in Finland on behalf of the large concern of precision tool manufacturers whom he represented. The family were then to move on to Sweden when, after further visits, they would return to the U.K. on the Gothenburg — Newcastle ferry.

Though David Jackson was a man who was used to travel, the sea voyage was an unfamiliar experience.

"Air travel is an essential parcel of a businessman's life but it does not offer any form of suspension from pressure. You never seem to catch up with yourself. No sooner have you got in the air than it's time to fasten your seat belts again," he reflected on a previous air trip to Scandinavia.

Transport drivers occupying passenger accommodation aboard the Finanglia service ships are usually accompanying a one-off load or vehicle. I was told that from time to time 'Enterprise' had carried vehicles as diverse as security vans, experimental buses, juggernaut excavators and racehorse boxes. Philip Rowe was the driver of a furniture van that contained the household effects of a British family who had moved to Central Finland.

He had driven aboard at Hull after a five-hour drive from Coventry. On arrival at Helsinki he faced a similar distance. In the meantime in his words it was to be "Feet up and a good book." This was not a regular event in his working lifestyle though he had made a trip to Germany two years earlier.

"Not bad this. A 3,000-mile round trip and I shall only drive 800," Philip Rowe added.

Each of these people was aboard 'Baltic Enterprise' for totally different reasons, but all had one immediate objective in common — to enjoy a short peaceful respite from the stresses and strains of every day life.

At times the opposing tracts of crew and passengers were more evident than others, none more so than at breakfast time. From the outset of the journey it became obvious that this part of the day was not the most opportune for social exchange between the two groups. But for the regular presence of seven passengers the gastronomic overture to the day would have been something of a 'non event.' Spasmodic appearances were made, essentially by the more senior officers, but excluding the Captain whose tray was taken to his quarters. Escaping the fussing of white-jacketed stewards in the saloon, the other officers preferred their bacon and eggs in a less formal mess-room one deck below.

As the day wore on we continued to purr our way across the North Sea amid brilliant sunshine. For the passengers deck chairs on the starboard bridge deck provided the greatest attraction. Tactfully sheltered from the airy breeze created by the ship's incessant forward motion, the chairs and loungers were lined up where the sun would flood down until late afternoon. The ritual of sun worshipping was occasionally broken by one of the participants surreptitiously rising and walking to the rail in anticipation of an on-coming ship or even the sight of land. There was no stampede when at such time a steward would arrive to announce that morning coffee was waiting in the passenger lounge or that the bar was open for lunchtime aperitifs. One by one the occupants of the chairs dragged themselves upright, slipped on a shirt or top and quietly, almost reluctantly, disappeared indoors.

For all that we were on the main Humber — Scandinavia lane the sea was almost devoid of traffic. Over midday I had looked in at the bridge. It was watch change-over time and both Second and Third Officers were present. The main topic between them was an expected mid-sea obstruction which, on our heading of 052 degress, we were steadily bearing down upon.

The North Sea is splattered with exploratory gas and oil rigs or production platforms. One of these ungainly structures was directly ahead some seven miles distant. It was clearly marked on the North Sea chart and Willie Maclaughlan had been observing it as a firm response on the radar for some time. Indeed, its arrival had proved 'Enterprise' to be within one cable of her expected course. Second Officer Bernard Elworthy's mandate on taking over the bridge watch was to side-step the ship to starboard allowing a comfortable margin of clearance.

His manipulation of the auto-pilot control was perceptible to the ear in the form of a rapid but muted click-a-click-a-click. Fixing a visual line

51

between our mast and the obstructing rig one could follow the interpretation of Elworthy's command by the computerised mechanism. Gradually the ship edged her nose away to the right until the pulsations from the auto-pilot suggested that the rudder was again being centralised. He joked on the slow if not lethargic mood in which the ship had accepted the brief course change.

"The tables are set for lunch, the drinks are on the bar and the weekend joint is ready for carving in the galley. I could have cleared the lot with a sharp starboard turn at this speed. I never have relished the thoughts of a 'keel hauling' though!"

I had recognised Bernard Elworthy as the young man who had courteously escorted me aboard the previous afternoon. He was bright in every sense of the word and obviously one filled with ambition.

"By pushing her over two degrees at this distance it saves making a tighter turn later. Even so we will soon have plenty of clear water to give that monstrosity a wide berth."

As he spoke, while following our angle through his binoculars from the starboard wing, the inner bridgehouse door opened. Like any conscientious Master, Gerry Brazendale was in the habit of making unscheduled appearances on his bridge. On this occasion I suspect he had detected the slight change of course and automatically found himself investigating the reason. Not that he showed mistrust in the actions of his Second Officer and not that he was unaware of the presence of the rig for it had been obstructing the main lane for some months. Inwardly Brazendale was a quiet family man with his roots firmly planted in the Dorset countryside. Six months of the year his profession placed him in a world alien to this domesticated existence; up to thirty-eight people, nine million pounds worth of ro-ro ship and three million pounds worth of cargo were his direct responsibility.

Elworthy did not rush forward with explanations; he had no need to. Neither did the Captain excite himself with questions; he knew that the ship had been steered carefully away from the obstruction. For the rest the chart table told him all he wanted to know; we were on course and on time. With an air of satisfaction he ambled across the expanse of bridgehouse carpet to join the young officer on the sundrenched wing.

Mid-afternoon we were confronted with a fellow ro-ro ship. Gleaming white topsides and a broad royal blue hull reflecting the brightness of the day, she gave every impression of a ship in her prime. I had been watching her from high on our 'monkey island' since she appeared from over the horizon but a few points to port. Tearing at an undecided sea, that parted in a plume of sparkling white spray in varying measures on either side of her bow, she conveyed the unseen picture of our own ship's indulgence. Obviously making approximately the same speed as ourselves and being on the reciprocal heading of 232 degrees the distance between the ships was soon cut down.

Abeam she displayed an array of containers as variegated in colour and markings as those that filled our own weather deck. In this profile her identity was revealed. Without the aid of glasses, the words TOR LINE, emblazoned in white against her soaring hull, were more than readable; and when showing her port quarter (on which a group of seamen were indiscriminately busy in the endless task of applying paint to weathered steel) TOR NERLANDIA, LONDON, was the announcement. Retracing our own steps back to the Humber I assumed her to be on the Gothenburg — Immingham service.

This small eventuality, which filled no more than fifteen minutes of the afternoon, would barely raise an eyebrow in either crew; yet, throughout, both teams were highly conscious of the meeting. Those who ramble on the hills and mountains register a similar nature of camaraderie. Remoteness, danger and hostility of surroundings promote a unity between men. When on high rocky ground battling through wind and rain complete strangers become bosom pals. They stop and pour out a wealth of goodwill — to share a Thermos, a cigarette and offer first-hand information of routes travelled. It's a sort of 'man against nature' event. Yet when the same meet in soft and verdant lowlands bathed with the warmth of day they accept the other's presence but pass by with barely a nod.

As in these lowlands, when positioned little more than twenty miles from land on a summer's day of light breezes and indifferent water, one would not expect high levels of excitement on meeting a similar vessel. Had we met after days of heavy weather many miles beyond the security of a friendly country undoubtedly the radio telephone would be buzzing and heads would be drawn to the rail.

It was early evening before Denmark was sighted. Showered, changed and contemplating a drink before the 6 p.m. dinner call, David Jackson and I were at the aft rail marvelling at the flight pattern of a dozen or so gulls that effortlessly slipstreamed the ship. Wings outstretched with never a beat they swooped and lifted around the stern forever maintaining the ship's pace. At first the land appeared as an obscure image almost beyond the horizon down the starboard side. A further five miles of wake had spread astern before the haze presented itself as an endless frontage of undulating sand-dunes.

To be specific this was the Province of Jutland, the bulky part of Denmark that assumes a narrow forty-five mile waistline at its border with Germany, that frontier being the only part of the country to be attached to the European mainland. Eighty miles away over our starboard quarter lay Esbjerg, the only deep-water port on Jutland's 250-mile North Sea coast. Esbjerg is one of the youngest townships in Denmark. Just over a hundred years ago no more than twenty people lived there, now the population is reaching 80,000. Apart from being the country's principal ferry link with the U.K., Esbjerg is the main gateway for imports and exports.

During our eighty-mile run in company with the Jutland coastline, there were times when its irregular contour brought us within view of the beaches and occasions when the shore completely disappeared. The ridge of dunes that backed these sweeping bights have been built through the ages by the strong westerlies driving in from the sea. Infrequently gaps in the sand hills were dotted with gaily painted houses, cottages and cabins that seemed to reach down to the tide-line.

Vorupor, Klitmoller and Hansted were names from the map that I placed on villages we sighted during the early evening. From a distance each seemed similar in character, the accent being unregimented grouping near the water's edge. The Jutland coastline receives a considerable influx of summer holidaymakers and recent years have seen a huge demand for sea-side retreats from business-weary Danes. State purchase along some of the finest stretches of shore has been followed by development of well-designed leisure villages. In wintertime the tourists are gone and the beaches deserted, the remaining population then being concentrated around the villages that harbour traditional fishing boats.

Here and there the continuity was broken where the dunes contrived themselves into sandy cliffs topped with tightly knitted woodland. Beyond one could see little, for the agricultural landscape that covers nine-tenths of Jutland rises barely above sea-level, especially on this western boundary. Hereabouts also lie large lagoons of inland water. These have been created by the strong winds beating back and ponding west-flowing streams. Nowhere in the whole of Denmark does the land rise more than 483 feet above sea-level, this point being Himmelbjerget (the Sky Mountain) in the Skanderborg region of Jutland.

For more than two hours that evening we followed a conventional freighter of approximately 10,000 gross tons. Shortly after meeting the Danish coast, Peter Green had changed our course to 065. This heading was to carry us to the northern-most tip of the country, named The Skaw. This is a sort of North Sea junction for ships on Scandinavian routes. The ship ahead was fixed on the very same heading as ourselves, obviously also making for The Skaw. Incessantly holding her eighteen and a half knots, 'Enterprise' slowly, very slowly consumed the differential and laboriously overhauled. Abeam of us this rather dank looking vessel displayed one of those unpronounceable Russian titles and the 'Hammer & Sickle' against her red-banded funnel.,

It was about this time that the ship developed a more pronounced 'roll,' apparently not an unexpected motion in these waters for even in summertime the meeting point of the Skagerrak, Kattegat and North Sea has a reputation for getting 'a little ruffled!' It wasn't a vicious roll but for the first time one became conscious of the need for hand rails along the alleyways, in the stairways and round the decks.

Apart from being renowned for the big seas that are so often a feature on its shores, Jutland gives its name to one of the most traumatic events in maritime history. On May 31st, 1916, a 400-square-mile segment of the North Sea between this point and the south-west coast of Norway staged the mightiest naval encounter on record — the Battle of Jutland, when the main fleets of Britain (149 ships) and Germany (116 ships) met head-on. After twelve hours of fury, destruction and confusion, the British Grand Fleet, under command of Admiral Sir John Jellicoe, had the German High

Seas Fleet retreating to the 'Fatherland.' However when losses were announced, Britain's toll of 6,000 lives and 14 sunken ships was almsot double that sustained by the Germans. The rejoicing was short-lived.

Dinner went by in a holiday mood. Sun-reddened faces, incessant chatter, gay summer prints and lightweight jackets were the passengers' contribution towards breaking the workaday atmosphere.

Suddenly the ship seemed alive with noise and colour. With both on-duty watch-keeping officers being briefly relieved for their evening sustenance, as many as sixteen people were seated at one time. Engineers, of whom little had been seen during the day, boosted their numbers. Excepting Chief Engineer Clive Buchan, who was a regular 'patron' of the dining saloon, the watch-keeping engineers found it unpractical to change from working suits to meet dress requirements of the saloon every mealtime. Dinner was the exception and they arrived uniformed as their fellow navigators in suitable open-necked white shirts with epaulets bearing gold-braided insignia of rank.

The Captain headed the middle of three tables which were sited in line across the room. In his company was a fair distribution of his officers and passengers. This arrangement also applied at the forward table headed by the Chief Engineer. The third of these eight-seat capacity tables was set aside for the junior officers, who, generally, were more punctual and consequently first to leave. Though uniforms were worn, mealtimes were informal. Usually the junior's table issued out a polite exchange of lively banter seemingly in complete oblivion to the Captain's presence. Having the Radio Officer in their midst this group was a principal source of up-to-date information. Between the inevitable bouts of talking shop either one or other officer seated elsewhere would realise that it was Saturday evening and sporting events would have been concluded for the day. Instinctively they would turn to the far table and, as though switching to B.B.C. 'Grandstand,' they could receive full coverage on either cricket scores, race winners or tennis results.

Though Brazendale subscribed to this desultory mode of conversation, one felt that his contribution was not deep rooted. His dialogue came in dutiful packages rather than from a sincere wish to be involved. The increased amount of 'roll,' which the passengers accepted with no more than a few high-spirited jokes, reminded him that the ship was steadily approaching The Skaw. To lesser acclaim The Skaw is something of an inverted 'Cape Horn.' Like that notorious South American landmark, the going can get rough there, exceedingly rough. But Brazendale was not plagued with thoughts of heavy weather; purely The Skaw, fortuitous to the 'Horn,' marked an important milestone and turning point on the outward route. Gone nightfall he would be on the bridge with his Third Officer to see the ship safely round.

When the coffee cups were empty the convivial atmosphere drifted through to the officers' smoke room. Much of the joviality was centred around a game of 'Scrabble' into which the Jackson family had been drawn by Electrical Officer George Hall. It seemed that through successive voyages George had notched up a long string of wins to his credit and finally choked his shipmates into distaste for the game. Now he had earned a reputation for badgering unsuspecting passengers into play. Needless to say the party of young men gathered around the room were firmly in support of the Jacksons — firstly offering over-the-shoulder advice to young Susan Jackson, then condemning the 28-year-old electrician's carefully chosen words as illegal!

Over the word game 'repartee' Chief Engineer Clive Buchan and Catering Officer John Garvey recaptured some of the high-spots of the ship's career for the benefit of Bob and Ruth Turnbull. Both these men had crewed 'Enterprise' since her maiden voyage, so much of the armchair sailing was first-hand issue. There were stories of force ten gales with waves that hit the ship like cannon fire; twisted radar aerials and furniture heaped against bulkheads, smashed deck gear and injured seamen.

Then there was Baltic ice with the ship ramming, screwing and tearing to free herself with every ounce of power she could muster. Icebreakers cutting freeways through one metre of pressure ice that closed in again within minutes.

"One winter night in the Baltic we met a northerly gale and punched it all the way to Helsinki. When the deck crew braved to venture to the foredeck at dawn they found that the continuous bludgeoning of big seas had left sea-spray that had frozen on every square inch of steel. In places this rime was almost one foot thick and it was estimated that we were coated with four hundred tons of the stuff." Clive Buchan called to Third Engineer Paul Davey at the bar who produced several colour photographs which clearly substantiated this claim. There was no end to these intriguing tales which passed this time of day for the following week.

The conversation at the bar was cars. Paul Davey disclosed intimate details of how he converted a wrecked Ford 'Pop' into a world-beating 'hot rod,' Philip Rowe's contribution being his exploits as a one-time car transporter driver.

Such was the way in which the evenings started. But all too soon the socialising was to diminish into a state of anticlimax. The workstyle of these mariners did not allow for an indefinite period of relaxation. Again watch-keeping cast a tight net of restraint among them. These who were scheduled for the eight to midnight stint were continually aware of the hour hand — drinks were out — there was insufficient time for board games. When relieved, the Chief Officer and Second Engineer would drop in for just the one drink, generally pass the time of day and with thoughts of a 4 a.m. watch would turn in for an early night. The hard part of the bargain did not rest entirely upon these watch-keepers. The Master, who was seldom seen socially in the smokeroom, would, from time to time, appear at the doorway and ask either Buchan or Garvey if they could 'spare a minute,' this being a polite opening to an hour spent over the inevitable pile of paperwork the Master has to contend with on every voyage. Electricians are indispensable on modern ships. Day workers they may be but the faults that they had to attend to are not fixed to an eight to five day.

George Hall could never guarantee on finishing his Scrabble game.

On the last haul along the Jutland coastline we took an off-shore glimpse of two seaside towns. Broaching the shore of a sandy promontory was Hirtshals. This is a small resort with a busy harbour. Apart from its age-long standing as a principal fishing port, Hirtshals is the Danish terminal for ferries that ply the Skagerrak from Kristiansand and Arendal in Southern Norway. By then the light was giving away to the orange glow of a gathering moon, leaving the view from the ship's starboard rail affording little of descriptive value.

Twenty-five miles further on we crept up on Skagen. In the daylight we would have seen a thriving resort thronged with summer holidaymakers. However at 11 p.m., this northernmost town of Denmark was represented by a widespread forest of twinkling lights that mirrored in the two miles of dividing ocean. In the 19th century Skagen was discovered by a fraternity of poets and artists. Its isolation and intensity of light fascinated them. Today the town's museum exhibits many fine paintings by artists that settled there. The habour at Skagen shelters a substantial fishing fleet, which is often supplemented by the arrival of Swedish trawlers seeking a fast rail connection to the German markets.

At The Skaw, 462 miles and 27 hours of sailing lay behind us. We had been told that after dark this 'lands end' would have nothing of visual interest to offer. But like the Turnbulls I was there and had to see for myself.

Beyond Skagen a two-mile spit of sandy ground terminates in a narrow point. The peninsula is crowned by the Grenen Lighthouse. Its 160 foot high tower has withstood the bludgeoning of winter gales since 1856. Other than this the headland is purely a summer tourist attraction for those who wish to see the ships go by.

We had not been misled for, away from the lighted backdrop of Skagen, only the powerful beam of the Grenen light gave evidence that we had levelled with The Skaw. Even then we did not turn a corner as one would have done at the corner of the High Street. On and on our mile-hungry ro-ro sailed until that light was weakening astern. There was much silver-glittered sea but little suggestion of land about us when a twenty degree call to starboard had our ranging bows heading towards waters new.

Though The Skaw had not provided the day with the finale that we had hoped for we were not to be dismayed. For out of a miniature constellation of moving ships appeared a belated 'prima-donna.' She came in the form of a large passenger ship heading westwards half-a-mile over to port. Decked with a tiara of glittering lights and moving in graceful silence she radiated all the charisma of a leading ballerina. We watched from the port rail and then ambled aft to see to her exit over the stern. We never discovered her name; it did not seem important — our day was complete.

CHAPTER FIVE

M.V. 'Baltic Enterprise' was built in the yards of Rauma-Repola Oy. On completion in mid-1973, it was said that she was the first ship to be built for British owners by a Finnish yard. Six months later her twin sister, 'Baltic Progress,' was placed second on the list. These two ships were the last in a line of five identical ro-ro's to be launched at Rauma. Apart from the original, 'Antares,' which was subsequently sold to other European interests, they were purpose-built for the U.K. — Finland Finanglia Ferries operation and have maintained this service since its inception.

Though, in these years, they have barely strayed off this route, to say that they have never operated between other ports would not be strictly true. In the case of 'Enterprise' there had been from time to time 'one off' calls embracing such places as Gothenburg, Halsingborg, Rotterdam, Antwerp and Gdynia. Likewise 'Baltic Progress' and the Finnish-owned 'Orion' have been involved in occasional diversions.

The main exception to this incessant 'ferrying' was in the case of the second of the Finnish-owned twins, 'Sirius.' During April 1976 there was a dock strike which involved all Finnish ports. Ships were arriving fully loaded and were not able to discharge. 'Enterprise,' for example, was trapped at Helsinki in this way for almost three weeks. At the time the effect of this disruption became reality, 'Sirius' was discharging at Hull. The Finland Steamship Company decided not to let their ship get tied up in this way and released her on charter for a 'one off' mission. One blustery April morning 'Sirius' left Hull in ballast bound for Montreal. On arrival at the Canadian seaport she loaded sectional buildings for the Middle East. This leg of the voyage brought her back across the Atlantic through the Mediterranean and Suez to the Red Sea port of Jedda. Returning to Hull, 'Sirius' had notched up 13,000 miles in a period of six weeks.

While on a recent visit to Hull I had the good fortune to meet Captain Claes Soderholm, senior Master of 'Sirius.' The trans-Atlantic voyaging came up in conversation and I learned that on the outward passage the great ocean had waged all its wrath against 'Sirius.'

"From rounding the North of Scotland to the approaches of Montreal the winds barely dropped below force ten gusting to force twelve. Riding high in ballast and with continuous south-westerlies thrusting mountainous seas at our port side we rolled heavily for ten full days. Believe me on stepping ashore in Canada we all staggered around as if we had just come off a rodeo 'bronco'!"

Though this had been an unpleasant journey one sensed that Captain Soderholm was justly proud of his green hulled ro-ro ship.

"She did all that we asked of her and proved that she was capable of operating through most extreme conditions."

When ships are built in batches they adhere to an area of uniformity that precludes any major individual characteristics. Externally the obvious distinguishing feature between the two Finnish ships and the U.B.C. sisters was the differential in house colours and marks. Structurally however all

58

four ships were identical to the last seam. Apparently there were some differences where the internal layout of the accommodation areas was concerned. In the main this was brought about to provide for the variation in staffing arrangements that exist between British and Finnish crewed ships.

Having Finnish birth-right, it was not surprising to find more than a gentle hint of Scandinavia integrated through the living area of 'Baltic Enterprise.' Without exception the furnishings, fittings and decor were to the high standard associated with such ancestry. Nowhere had the comfort and well-being of officers, passengers and crewmen been overlooked. Without being frilly or fussy the interior incorporated a fair share of the refinements that determine sea-going luxury — functional comforts rather than overbearing sumptuousness.

Taking the 'monkey island' as the top-most level and crew's quarters on the main deck as the lower, the superstructure of the ship could be said to comprise five decks. Essentially all the accommodation was encompassed within the superstructure. This left the hull entirely free for cargo, engines and ancillary systems. Up top the 'monkey island' was no more than the deck-head to the bridgehouse and adjacent rooms situated on the Navigating Bridge Deck. It was a deck purely in a pedestrian sense — it contained no buildings or offered any shelter — strictly a place for oceans of fresh air and unimpeded views, nothing else.

Within the bridgehouse one felt the true width of the ship. Observing the nagivators constantly pacing between chart table and radar console, and from wing to wing, I deduced that this was no occupation for those who frowned upon distance walking. Spread across the rear bulkhead of this capacious nerve-centre were three internal doors through which could be found a toilet, the main stairway and the Captain's 'sea cabin' respectively. The 'sea cabin' was a small room sparingly furnished with a settee-bed, bookshelves, table and chair. The Master would use this temporary accommodation during long spells of bad weather when his presence on the bridge is required at all times. Beyond the central self-closing door a U-shaped landing opened the way to the Radio Room and Radio Officer's quarters to port. As to the equivalent space to starboard there was a door from which a level pitched whine was perpetually emitted. Here I was shown a room which housed the internal telephone exchange plus banks of impressive electronic instruments akin to the radar, gyro compass and other scientific gadgetry upon which a modern ship relies.

Away from the weather deck which was strictly a working area, the Navigating Bridge Deck offered more open deck space than any other. Running abaft of the bridge wings were broad deck walkways that provided a marginal level of shelter from the headway winds. Consequently this deck was most favoured by the passengers as somewhere to spread their deck chairs and sun-loungers.

Descending the blue panelled stairway that led from the bridgehouse, one was confronted with a wall display in the form of a large Admiralty chart covering both North and Baltic Seas. Purely for decorative purposes

An area of one of the spacious forward facing passenger cabins.

One of the four starboard side passenger cabins.

it had been carefully coloured in and boldly marked with the courses the ship plies between Hull and the Finnish ports.

The Bridge Deck, one level below the bridgehouse, contained the main living area of the Captain, Chief Engineer and passengers. This was, of course, the most elegant accommodation aboard and it was so arranged as to take full advantage of the ship's generous beam. The Master's quarters, which comprised sleeping, bathroom, lounge and office areas, were laid out in an 'L' shaped fashion at the starboard leading corner of the block. The Chief Engineer was accommodated correspondingly at the port corner and like the Captain enjoyed natural light through forward and side-facing windows.

Filling a prodigious amount of space that spread between these suites was a pair of 'king-sized' two-berth passenger cabins. To use the term 'roomy' here would under-emphasise the volume of these cabins but to say that each covered a floor area that normally would be taken up by three or four ferry ship cabins would not be far from accurate. As sole occupant of the starboard hand mentioned apartment for the duration of the voyage, I welcomed the space available for use as a working base. Linking its widespread walls was a patterned royal blue carpet with which the remainder of the soft furnishings blended. The two oversized single berths, bunks or beds, whichever you choose to name them, were covered with continental quilts — a convenience appreciated by the cabin stewards. There was what seemed to be sufficient drawer, cupboard and wardrobe space to swallow the luggage of the Royal Household and, apart from a cleverly designed dressing table that converted to a writing desk, a table and loose chairs were provided. The decor, like many areas of the ship, was based upon simulated hessian wall panels together with rich sapele woodwork. The 'en suite' toilet, lined in hard laminate panels with Scandinavian pine ceiling, was fitted with w.c., washbasin and shower. There was what seemed an endless supply of piping hot water at all hours of the day. Concealed lighting both within the white panelled deck-head and behind the full-width window pelmet gave soft but adequate illumination.

On the debit side the cabin held but one disappointment — the view from the two forward facing windows was badly obstructed. While at sea the huge weather deck gantry crane was parked and locked in a position close to the forward end of the superstructure. Its massive cross-beam winged athwart ships in direct line of the Bridge Deck forward cabins. Subsequently one had the option of peering above the structure to acquire a view of the heavens or beneath to see a colourful but uninteresting array of deck cargo. For anyone unlike myself who wished to spend the lion's share of the voyage in his own company this could probably be an irritating factor. For me the cabin was a place for work and rest. This I did in more than ample comfort.

The four cabins so far described led out onto a broad alleyway that ran the full width of the accommodation block. Fixed centrally on its dark brown panelled bulkhead was a beautifully etched sheet of glass. Discreetly illuminated this decoration featured a fully rigged Ship of the Line, a

The dining saloon looking aft.

Dining saloon mural depicts maritime history of Hull.

nineteenth century paddle steamer and a profile of 'Baltic Enterprise' super-imposed against a dark coloured background in the form of a map of Scandinavia. The effect of this was most pleasing and being prominently displayed won much admiration from the passengers.

As in all areas of the Bridge Deck the alleyways were carpeted wall to wall. Two such warmly covered corridors ran aft from the main stair-head concourse. Over the starboard side this provided access to four more passenger cabins and a small infrequently used sitting room. The port side alleyway led to the dining saloon, the steward's serving pantry and, aftermost, a lounge where passengers could while away abundant sea-borne hours.

Although only half the size of the forward suites, the four starboard side passenger cabins incorporated the very same amenities without appearing overcrowded. Each enjoyed sea views through a single window overlooking the Bridge Deck walkway. The compact layout seemed to inspire a cosiness that the larger cabins lacked — a feature probably much more appreciated on a long ice-bound winter voyage.

The sitting room was distinctly furnished with a large circular mahogany table, six occasional chairs, a wall-fixed settee and an impressive floor to ceiling wall unit that contained board games, books and the like. The 'out on a limb' location of this room seemed to dissuade any regular visitations other than those of the stewards armed with vacuum cleaner and duster.

Measuring thirty feet by sixteen the dining saloon was by far the largest room of the accommodation block. Here soft furnishings were in blending tones of sage green and mustard, while the main decor was again based on sapele woodgrain panels together with the restful oatmeal colour of hessian-covered walls. Overlooking the port side and feeding natural light into the saloon were six rectangular windows — two at the end of each across-ships table. Directly opposite, and dominating the long inner wall, was a fifty-six square foot mural depicting the maritime history of Hull. With ambitious use of colour, its creator, Keith Hemsby, had formulated a kaleidoscope of ships, landmarks and prominent figures covering the heydays of the port, much the largest inset being a side profile of 'Baltic Enterprise' herself. This ran the full length across the mural base.

Tables were permanently covered in snow-white linen and a type-written menu was placed at each every meal time. Excepting special arrangements made for duty officers, meal schedules were tightly adhered to, breakfast being 08.00, lunch 12.00 and dinner 18.00.

For all that menus were generally based on traditional English fare, the choice of dishes remained surprisingly varied throughout the duration of the voyage. On a typical day, breakfast, naturally, was well supplied with fruit juices, cereals, sausage, bacon with eggs done in the usual variety of ways. Sometimes there would be smoked haddock or kippered herrings. Always tea and coffee flowed generously to round off an ample quota of toast and marmalade.

For lunch one could expect soup of the day and an entree of fish or perhaps egg mayonnaise. For main course there was always choice of hot or cold dishes — roast pork, lamb chops or ham salad all served with the usual vegetables and trimmings. Peach melba, apple pie with ice cream would follow, together with the never-empty coffee pot.

On such a day the dinner menu would advertise such delights as salmon fish cake with parsley sauce; chicken casserole or mixed grill with Norfolk turkey as a cold dish. Banana split, fruit pudding or trifle would follow for sweet.

These menus stood in both officers' dining room and the seamen's mess. Regardless of captain or pantry boy everyone aboard was served the same choice of food.

Morning coffee and afternoon tea broke the interval between main meals. For passengers this was served in their own small lounge situated directly aft of the dining saloon pantry. At the given time the duty steward would quietly move through the tiny congregation of travellers and place loaded trays upon a spacious centrally fixed coffee table. The ladies in the party would then 'jockey' for the privilege of playing 'mum' — normally

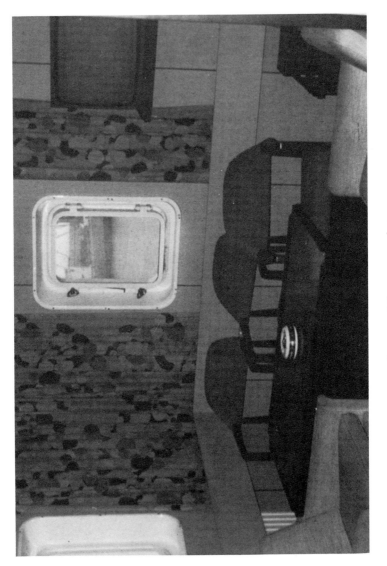

A corner of the passenger lounge.

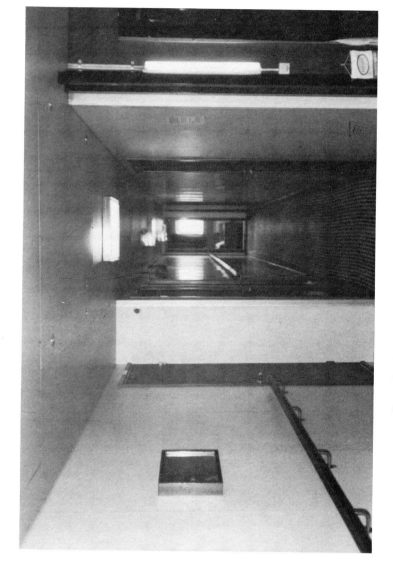

Port-side alleyway looking aft to the passenger lounge.

making sure that the unaccompanied were first to be served. The tea, coffee and hot water would flow endlessly from the silver-plate pots while biscuit plates were passed around in indiscriminate fashion.

Sandwiched between three substantial main meals these light refreshments came more as a nicety than a necessity; brief social interludes to the relaxed daytime routine rather than to provide secondary sustenance.

Though pleasantly furnished with a three-piece lounge suite, several occasional chairs and a mahogany sideboard unit, the room never induced an air of cosiness. Primarily this was due to an external doorway that provided direct access through the aftermost bulkhead to the outer deck. During the run of good weather the lounge became something of a passageway for the door was almost continually open. On indifferent days those seeking a breath of sea air would unavoidably allow a blast of cold air to circle the room as they hurried to close the portal.

Appropriately a wall-mounted clock in the stairway between Bridge and Boat Decks showed British Summer Time. Whether summer or winter ship's time was always fixed on B.S.T.; in effect this halved the two-hour differential between Greenwich Mean and Finnish time. While in Finland the ship's clocks read one hour late — at U.K. ports in wintertime they were one hour early.

When on the Boat Deck, one could be said to be in the heart of the ship's accommodation. Here eight officers were housed — five in forward cabins overlooking the weather deck and three down the starboard side. The alleyways ran in unison with those on the Bridge Deck, but their decor came in more striking contrasts — two-tone blue for the walls or bulkheads while above the deckhead was in bright orange. Carpet runners stretched the full fifty-foot length of the fore-aft passages, which were permanently lit by flush overhead fitments.

Space allotted for the individual apartments was related to seniority of rank or the role they had to fulfill. Nevertheless each officer enjoyed more than sufficient elbow room in smart surroundings. All the Boat Deck cabins had their own private facilities including a sitting area that contained refinements such as a drinks refrigerator and concealed lighting. In common with many ship owners of standing, U.B.C. allow wives of officers to accompany on a limited number of voyages each year. Consequently the sleeping area in Boat Deck cabins contained a double bed.

The ship's office and liquor bond store were located at opposite ends of the starboard alleyway.

Filing cabinets containing an accumulation of ship's records made up the bulk of the office furniture. Unattended behind a closed door for most of the time, it was more a registry than a place of commercial activity. One fitment worthy of note was a Telecom 'pay phone.' On docking in the U.K. this was quickly linked to the normal Telecom grid, allowing crew to dial home direct from the ship.

Away from port the bond locker was a much busier enterprise. Here, while the ship was at sea, beers, wines, spirits and cigarettes were sold under the strict control of the Catering Officer at off-duty prices. In response to

Bar in the officers' smoke room.

my inquisitiveness John Garvey readily unlocked a stout woodgrain door adjacent to his Boat Deck quarters. Inside I saw strong white wood racks heavily loaded with box upon box of canned beers and lagers. An even more heavily secured portal gave access to the inner sanctum. Reverently lined in the cool interior were tidy rows of corrugated cases containing scotch, sherry, table wines and the like — cigarettes came in a wide variety of brands neatly shelved in packs of two hundred. I was told that the sale of spirits was restricted to officers and passengers. The seamen's tipple was confined to beer or lager excepting when 'paying off' the ship. Then they were allowed to purchase the normal duty-free quota.

Originally the officers' smoke room was 'dry.' The copper-topped bar came as an improvement though the ingenuity of several members of the crew. Effectively set across one corner of the fourteen by twelve foot room it helped to conjure up the atmosphere one expects to find in the local pub 'cosy.' Before the advent of the bar, drinking (such as it is on short sea voyages) had been a disorganised pursuit, each man having to buy his own stock. Now the port side smoke room was their social centre and although it was originally intended solely for their own use they normally opened a warm invitation to all passengers. Bar duties were carried out by the officers themselves on a roster that worked in with the normal watch system. Compared to inflationary shore costs, prices at the 'Enterprise' bar were ridiculously low. Even so small profits were made sufficient to provide extra items for the room — latest records, tapes, books and games. The remainder was regularly donated to various charitable organisations, the R.N.L.I. and children's homes being among the beneficiaries mentioned.

A few paces further aft along the port side alleyway was the officers' mess room. As mentioned this fitted as an alternative eating place for those who were unable to forfeit sufficient time to change for the more dressy Bridge Deck saloon. Covers on the two six-seat tables came in blue and white gingham while the stainless steel chairs were upholstered in bright orange p.v.c. This was definitely a place of their own, somewhere to lett off steam a private den where blunt and earthy banter could flow across the table without caution. Adorning the cream finished walls and adding to the air of masculinity was a well-used dart board and, naturally, the usual 'girlie' calendar.

Next door a complete contrast — indeed a place where these men had something to get steamed up over.

Coming from Finnish stock, 'Enterprise' had inherited part and parcel of the national constitution — the sauna. The generous amount of space that the architects had put aside for the installation of a sauna (correctly pronounced 'sowna,' the *sow* as in female pig) gave a strong indication of the importance the Finns place upon this form of relaxation. Having the traditional pine cabin hot room built within a complex that included three shower cubicles, washbasin, toilet, changing and rest areas it compared to any well-equipped shore sauna. Normally the officers used this amenity in small groups during the evening or night depending on watch commitments. Passengers were free to use the sauna during the daytime and a reservation board was provided for those wishing to make a 'date.' An additional piece of equipment within the changing area was a gymnasium style rowing machine. This had been provided through the generosity of a Finnish passenger who obviously felt that the crew were in need of some extra exercise!

Completing the Boat Deck accommodation was a small laundry. This windowless room, situated aft of the sauna, was furnished with two twin-tub washing machines, a large stainless steel sink, ironing boards along with the usual requisites found in a launderette. On the far wall a door led into an ever-hot drying room that was threaded from side to side with overhead clothes lines. The laundry was intended to enable each officer to keep up to date with small items of washing that accumulate after a week or so at sea. The main bulk of the ship's laundry, bed and table linen, was collected by contractors each time she docked at Hull.

Probably no more has been written about a ship's accommodation than that of Cunard's 'Queen Elizabeth 2.' The chapters of superlatives are so comprehensive it would be difficult to add to them without some degree of repetition. Neither, having seen the main public rooms aboard that floating palace, would I consider drawing comparisons alongside any other ship I have been acquainted with, let alone a hard-working ro-ro freighter. Yet, through having a topical 'spin off,' the circumstances under which my wife, daughter and I had the privilege of stepping aboard the 'greatest ship afloat' purely as observers come vividly to mind.

In this instance the word 'privilege' should not be taken lightly, for, in these days of vandalism, extremist groups and bomb scares, it is far from normal practice for the general public to be accepted up the Q.E.2 gangway as visitors. Indeed the two-hour guided tour was the culmination of almost two months of correspondence and telephone calls, in the first instance to the Cunard offices at Southampton and latterly to head office in London.

The idea of seeing Q.E.2 was sparked off after we had arranged to take a family holiday in the New Forest area. Knowing that the ship would be arriving at Southampton after completing a Caribbean cruise during the period of our vacation, I contacted Cunard's Public Relations Department expressing my long-standing wish to see the vessel. Promptly the postman delivered a sympathetic reply firmly indicating that under no circumstances, due to security reasons, were visitors allowed aboard. Enclosed were a number of glossy brochures advertising the liner's forthcoming world cruise. Here, I assumed, was a tactful way of suggesting that if I was so interested in Q.E.2, why not circumnavigate the globe aboard her?

Undaunted by the rebuff from Southampton, I wrote to a senior director of the company enclosing a copy of one of my articles as authentic proof of my interest in shipping. On this occasion the request was received cautiously but more favourably and, following a telephone conversation to fill in details of the visit and of my wife and daughter who were to accompany me, I was finally granted permission to go aboard; boarding passes would be sent direct from Southampton. There followed a three-week period of total silence by Cunard, leaving only five clear days before our journey south. At this stage I embarked on a marathon of anxious telephone calls both to London and Southampton with the result that only twenty hours before the pending visit did I receive verbal instructions on how to find the person holding our boarding passes.

Our arrival at the Ocean Terminal that warm Sunday morning was in unison with hundreds of passengers and well-wishers for the ship was due to sail for New York within three hours. Kindly hostesses approached asking whether we were travelling or there simply to wave goodbye. My replies were met with a succession of courteous disbelief.

"No-one ever goes aboard just to look over Q.E.2; passengers only I'm afraid. Are you in possession of boarding passes?"

"No," I sighed. "But I was expecting to meet your Mr. 'X' who was bringing them along."

"I'm sorry, but Mr. 'X' isn't here today. Visitors used to be taken over the ship in conducted parties but all that finished after the 1972 mid-Atlantic bomb scare. I just can't help you — sorry."

No-one seemed aware of the rare concession that had been sanctioned by the top-brass of the company, neither was the gentleman that I had been instructed to find at the terminal. All the weeks of negotiation seemed to have fallen to nothing until, after fifteen hapless minutes of searching through the crowded departure hall, we came face to face with a uniformed young woman holding the three precious passes. Pat, once a senior guide and courier aboard the Q.E.2 during the era of day visitors, had been called out especially that very morning to show us through the glittering interior. However, our sighs of relief were held in suspension when our guide explained that even at that 'eleventh hour' all was not certain that we would get aboard. A lightning strike by crane drivers had stopped the regular gangway from being used.

After some confusion a temporary gangway was opened up at the stern of the ship and, amidst the steady stream of embarking passengers, we finally trod the prime Burma teak of the after-deck. During the two hours allocated we waded our way across the lush carpets of the many lounges, dining rooms, cocktail bars and the most luxurious (and expensive!) state-rooms afloat — a breath-taking experience to say the least.

Back in the terminal building, literally minutes before departure time, our host, regaining her normal heart-rate, commented that although our visit was relatively short we had probably seen more of the ship than the average passenger on a one-month cruise. Pat told us that on one occasion when she arrived at the terminal there was a party of Royal children waiting to be shown over the ship. But apart from such V.I.P. guests, to her knowledge, we were only the second party of visitors to step aboard since the big security clampdown. Indeed it was a privilege.

Our visit to Southampton dockland was rounded off in an unscheduled but convivial way. While strolling back to the car after watching Q.E.2 sedately ease away from the quayside to the uplifting strains of Elgar's

'Pomp and Circumstance,' I noticed a cream funnel broaching the skyline in another area of the waterfront. Shortly it became obvious that the motif embellishing the side of this funnel was that of U.B.C. Recollecting that the Company had recently opened up a cargo only service between Southampton, Bordeaux and Bilbao in the wake of the Swedish Lloyd passenger ferry 'Patricia,' I assumed the ship to be m.v. 'Goya,' a 3,779 gross tons ro-ro, specially purchased to inaugurate the run. Some of the officers who had been posted to the ship I knew from old so I threaded the car through a maze of dockland in pursuit.

'Goya' had docked early that morning on completion of a week-long stormy round voyage across the Bay of Biscay. A number of officers were assembled in the ship's bar enjoying a pre-lunch drink when we 'descended' upon them. We were given a cordial reception not the least by Chief Officer Duncan Glass (ex Second Officer of 'Baltic Enterprise') with whom we spent an entertaining hour chatting over a shipboard beer. Much of the conversation ran over comparisons between 'Goya' and 'Enterprise.' 'Goya' was of the breed of ro-ro's with forward superstructure. It raised almost directly from the bow and ran aft for a third of the ship's 144 metres. Our host explained that this allowed totally unobstructed vision from the bridge and, with the engines being situated deep down in the hull way aft of the accommodation, a quiet and vibration-free ride. However for tight manoeuvring situations which are commonplace for short-haul ro-ro's he felt that aft superstructure and control vessels were by far superior.

"When docking a ro-ro, invariably one has to go astern to meet the loading ramp. On a ship such as 'Goya' almost 150 yards separate the controls from that crucial point," said Glass. Additionally the forward superstructure met with a great deal of criticism when the ship was steaming into head seas.

"The accommodation takes the full brunt of the pitching. In the 'Bay' this can be severe and often. Occasionally we have to resort to strapping ourselves into our bunks — meals become a shambles. Furthermore the instrumentation on the bridge is subjected to considerable stress and subsequently requires frequent re-calibration."

Accepting noise and vibration as a secondary consideration the general preference among the ex 'Enterprise' and 'Progress' men grouped around the bar ran towards ships with superstructure sited at the after end.

Due to cancellation of an order, 'Goya' had been bought by U.B.C. at an incomplete stage from a Rumanian yard as a stop-gap vessel. She had been towed to Kiel, cut in two and lengthened with an additional mid section. This resulted in her being slightly longer than 'Enterprise' but fourteen feet less generous in beam.

In comparing the standard of accommodation they all agreed that the Finnish-built ships were by far superior.

"There is little doubt that on the Finnish service ships we were spoiled. Excepting modern supertankers it is unlikely that many cargo freighters boast better accommodation."

Officers on each U.B.C. ro-ro ship took leave on a 50-50 basis. Usually this meant that each man completed three round voyages then took leave for the equivalent amount of time. Consequently the ships had complement of officer to form two complete crews. These crews did not change over en bloc. Therefore on completion of a voyage there was always one or two men leaving the ship and newcomers arriving to step into their shoes.

The seaman's leave was less generous — they worked a two-voyage on, one-voyage off basis, each man spending eight months of every year aboard to the officers' six.

The fifteen seamen aboard 'Baltic Enterprise' were housed on the Main Deck. This represented the 'ground floor' of the accommodation block.

Each man had his own separate cabin which, though less spacious and palatial than the afore-mentioned, was smartly furnished with a single berth, storage units, table and chair and also incorporated a h.c. washbasin. The Bo'sun and Senior Cook had the additional amenity of an en-suite shower and toilet. From the port side alleyway they had access to the combined dining and recreation room, a laundry and a fully equipped sauna complex. Again, colour schemes were biased towards contrasting combinations of blue, orange and oatmeal with widespread use of hard laminate surfaces, as throughout the ship sapele woodgrain internal doors being the norm.

Living space on the Main Deck was less spacious than elsewhere. Internally the clinically clean galley with its attendant dry and refrigerated stores absorbed a substantial portion of the after end. Outdoors a broad throughway, allowing vehicular access between weather and after decks down the starboard side, took a considerable slice off the block at that level.

Several monochrome television sets were dotted around the accommodation. Though intended to receive a wide range of continental channels, reception was greatly limited and inconsistent. On leaving U.K. shores the picture very soon diminished beyond legibility. In Baltic waters Swedish television programmes sometimes came loud and clear. But often viewing was spoiled as the ship moved further and further away from the transmitter.

On such occasions a succession of irate viewers would leave their chairs to work on the control knobs unsuccessfully attempting to clear an ever-advancing 'snow storm.'

"This always happens at a crucial part of the programme," exclaimed an angry George Hall one night. He was one in a group of smoke room clientele watching the final 'shoot-out' in a western film through a ferocious spell of interference.

I was not unduly perturbed, neither were the rest of the passengers. After all we hadn't gone to sea to watch T.V.

CHAPTER SIX

More than one hundred sea miles south of The Skaw, the Kattegat's expansive waters narrow abruptly until its outlying shores merge together to within two miles. From the east, Sweden awakens to the channel in a seemingly endless green ribbon of shore-struck conifers. Hereabouts, on the westward flank, Denmark's contribution is none the more spectacular. Occasional clusters of beach bungalows leisurely spread afront of the pines offer relief to an otherwise featureless onshore panorama. The land here is in fact Zealand — the largest of Denmark's numerous islands and most populated acreage.

At 05.30 in brilliant early sunshine, 'Baltic Enterprise' thrust her 452 foot long bulk centrally along the narrowing wedge of water. Throughout the early hours of Sunday we had poured down the Kattegat leaving Gothenburg, Varberg and Falkenberg to port while the tiny islands of Laeso and Antholt were likewise discarded unseen beyond our starboard quarter. Around the 04.00 watch change-over we had been put on a heading of 162 degrees and it was that course that carried us headlong towards the funnel-neck called 'The Sound.'

Captain Brazendale had risen early to join his Chief Officer on the bridge watch. Both, lightly dressed in shirt-sleeves and sporting dark glasses against a low but reflectively powerful sunlight, paced intermittently between the bridge facia, chart table and the floodlit port wing. Rightly Brazendale was never in the habit of making a social occasion out of his business on the bridge. Certainly the hour did not help to promote a flood of conversation to flow between the two navigators. It had gone without saying that the Master's presence was due to the fact that we were rapidly approaching a forty-mile stretch of busy and often congested waterway. His business was to pilot his ship through these difficult reaches until such time as the fairway opened up to the Baltic Sea. Though Green had guided 'Enterprise' accurately to the mouth of the 'Sound' he had automatically and unquestionably assumed the role of Brazendale's aide.

"I think we will have a man up on the wheel now, Peter."

Brazendale eventually broke a long silence having made an extensive probe of the silver-blue water beyond the ship's head. Green quietly moved over to the internal phone and dialled the crew's quarters.

"One six five, please," was the call three minutes later as the duty seaman settled behind the wheel.

In anticipation Green was at the auto-pilot control effecting the change-over to manual.

"Steady one six five, sir."

Still holding the eighteen and a half knots that we had adopted on leaving the Humber, we shoved forward into the Sound.

Nine miles further on and thirty minutes later the rumbling of 'Enterprise's exhausts ricocheted over a shimmering waterway flanked by the buildings of two towns. Halsingborg in Sweden and Helsingor on the Danish shore face each other across the narrowest reach of the Sound.

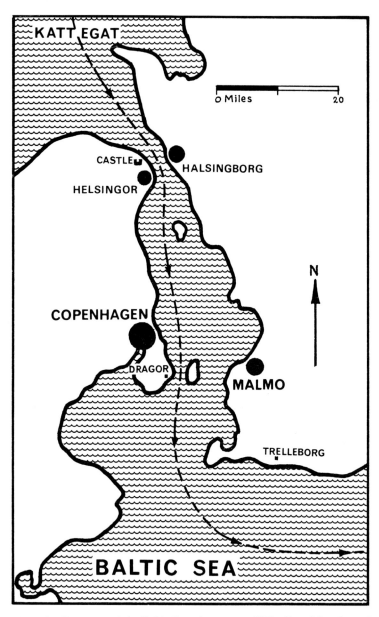

Linking the Kattegat and the Baltic Sea, the waters of 'The Sound' break on the shores of Denmark to the west and Sweden to the east.

Kronborg Castle, Helsingor.

77

Throughout the day small car ferries ply continuously between the two centres. In addition countless summertime pleasure craft take advantage of the spaciousness of these sheltered waters. As at all times, vigilance is the operative word for those on the bridge of large commercial vessels making a through passage.

On the first stages of our passage along the Sound, good fortune had smiled upon our navigators. Following my almost nocturnal observations through the angled screens of the wheelhouse I had made for the open air of the 'monkey island.' From there, apart from a number of early morning sailors weaving dinghies close by the shore, the view was one of an unimpeded road of flat silver sea reaching between the two countries until it merged with an empty sky many miles ahead.

The most striking event on approaching Helsingor was the sighting of Kronborg Castle. The castle, which is world famous through being the setting of Shakespeare's 'Hamlet,' was sited on a low promontory that allowed the waters of the Sound to lap within feet of its base. It has stood there since completion in 1583 though a serious fire put it close to destruction in 1629. A restoration programme was carried out later by one of Denmark's favourite kings — Christian IV. Kronborg has innumerable treasures; furniture, paintings, tapestries, carved doorways. There is a 200 foot long banqueting hall, a maritime museum and a chapel which is still used for marriages.

Beyond the sunlit ramparts and green copper pinnacles of Kronborg, Helsingor was set on rising land pleasantly decked with broad leaf trees. Helsingor flourished during the 13th century when the sea route to the Baltic round The Skaw came into common use. 'Sound' dues were imposed and a bronze cannon was used to enforce this levy. This situation continued until 1857 when the Danes agreed to abolish taxes in return for a cash payment of £4,000,000 by maritime nations. The cannon stands on a platform beneath the castle walls; unfortunately I was unable to see it from the rail of our hurrying ro-ro. On the other hand it was fortunate that we did not hear it!

Through a nautical 'one way' system, 'Enterprise's' course at this stage favoured the Danish shore leaving the opposite bank best viewed through binoculars. Here sleeping Halsingborg stood embellished with the aurora of morning light. A thousand years ago this city was an important European capital. Today it is a thriving port and industrial centre of some 80,000 inhabitants and the eighth largest city in Sweden. Within its precincts Halsingborg displays vast contrasts of architecture, notably medieval towers, 18th century palaces and mansions together with a fair share of ultramodern designs.

The dock area was, of course, a prominent feature on the water-front. Neatly spaced along the harbour walls were dozens of tall white flag-poles. I was told that when a ship enters Halsingborg a flag, representative of her country of origin, is hoisted. On that occasion all the poles were bare. Obviously all the flags ware taken down at night and not hoisted again until some sensible hour!

Peter Green told me that 'Enterprise' had called at Halsingborg on just one occasion. This short diversion while on her regular Finnish service was to discharge a consignment of Sweden-bound touring caravans.

Shortly the twin towns were falling astern. While I pondered at the rail over their gradual withdrawal, ferry boats pulled out to cross the Sound from either shore. The time was 06.10 and I expected that these were the first ferries of the day. Danes and Swedes continually cross to each other's territory and the numerous ferry routes between the two countries carry upwards of 15,000,000 passengers annually. The Halsingborg bound ferry wasted no time in crossing astern of us, dissecting the road of foaming wake we embossed along the channel.

Having by then sailed 590 nautical miles and 35 hours out of Hull, we were past the half-way stage to Helsinki. From time to time I would hear, below me, Brazendale call course changes to the helmsman — 178 — 180 — 183. Being bound for one of the world's northernmost capitals this temporary dash due south seemed somewhat bizarre. From then on the 'Sound' became more and more spacious. Happily, as the two shorelines progressively opened up, the buoyed channel that we followed carried us within viewing distance and parallel to the Danish seaboard. Often we passed close by islands and islets. Some had small holiday cabins perched among groves of fresh green conifers, others were no more than rocky outcrops poking through the surface. One island alone fell into a category totally uncharacteristic to a peaceful Sunday morning scene. Amid a tranquil sea sprinkled with the gently filling sails of leisure seekers' yachts and dinghies lay an island fortress of modern defence systems. Rising from the rocky terrain of this waterborne stronghold, named Middlegrund, were plinths of concrete bearing fearsome ballistic missiles that pointed in each and every direction. Not a place to dwell upon; in fact somewhere left well astern — which it soon was.

By 07.15, still hauling southwards, we were abeam of Copenhagen. Rising from land barely a few feet above sea-level, Denmark's capital, viewed from the sea, gave me an impression of a northern Venice. Though more than a mile away the skyline was as clear as it was varied. This was an assortment of modern commercial high-rise buildings amid the coppered roofs and golden spires of architectural masterpieces. It is often asked why the capital of Denmark should be situated on the extreme edge of Zealand on the country's eastern seaboard. The answer is that historically Copenhagen was the capital of Norway, Southern Sweden and other Baltic territories. This kingdom was known as The Union of Kalmar. Being a well-sheltered port with easy access to the high seas, Copenhagen was an ideally located capital.

From a small village in the 11th century, Copenhagen steadily grew in size and importance and in the 15th century the King went to live there. With the accession of King Christian IV (1588-1648) the then prosperous city entered into a great period of expansion. Christian was a man of extraordinary energy and was possesssed with a passion for building. He was responsible for many of the Renaissance style buildings that we could pick out from the decks of our ship. Copenhagen is now the home of over one million Danes, which represents one quarter of the country's population. It is the largest of the Scandinavian capitals.

All too soon the six miles of quays and installations that faced the main waterway were falling beyond our starboard quarter. However our sustained contact with the shoreline brought reward through our approach to the main runway of Copenhagen's International Airport at Kastrup. The eastern extremity of the broad tarmac with its battery of approach lights pushes out towards the water until the tideway almost licks at the undercarriages of landing aircraft. Indeed, had we been on a more westerly heading at that particular time, we would have needed landing wheels down too! What seemed one of the most timely incidents of the voyage was the arrival of a Boeing 747 nigh to the time 'Enterprise' levelled across the end of the runway. It momentarily cast an enormous shadow over the ship. Simultaneously the roar of its jets temporarily muted the relentless bark offered by our funnel top.

The airport is situated on Amager, a pear-shaped island that is linked to Copenhagen by its harbour bridges. Together with Malmo Airport ten miles across the Sound (at the time of writing) Kastrup has reached its operational limit. In solution it has been proposed to develop a new joint international airport on the mid-Sound island of Saltholm. The plan includes a four-mile tunnel to Denmark while a six-mile bridge would link the island to Sweden.

No sooner had the noise of the aircraft landings subsided when there was an abrupt change in the attitude of the ship. The concurrent sounds and pulsations created through continually muscling at full service speed had become an integral part of a ship's make-up, insomuch as one's senses become dulled or even, to some degree, oblivious to their existence. Only when this chain frequency is broken or changed does one become fully awake to its monotony.

'Enterprise's' rhythm had changed from a quickstep to a slow foxtrot. We had arrived at the Drogden Channel where, on a visually vast expanse of water, the marks and buoys had appreciatively narrowed the nagivational fairway. Brazendale had cut our headway by more than half for not only was there less elbow room but we were suddenly among other traffic. Ahead and approaching was a freighter of some considerable tonnage that was following in the wake of a deeply laden coaster. Astern was a large car ferry which like ourselves was making for the Baltic, while creeping down our port side was a pair of small tugs. They were coping with a huge box-square lighter piled as high as a house with what appeared to be timber enough to build a 'Noah's Ark.'

"One hell of a pile of matchsticks," was Brazendale's comment after offering a cursory wave to the tugmen.

The Drogden Channel lies between coastal banks which extend from both Saltholm and Ameger. The name Drogden is of ancient Dutch origin and alludes to the diminished depths in the channel. In places it is no more than eight metres deep. The channel carried us past the attractive watersedge village of Dragor on Amager Island. And as we were closer to the shore than at any time during the Sound passage, we had a fine view over the picturesque marina and harbour there. Dragor is a terminal for ferries from and to Skanor at the south-west tip of Sweden.

Ten miles beyond Drogden the Sound gave way to the southern reaches of the Baltic Sea. Here the ship re-established her mood of urgency arrowing her white, roller bow wave south-eastwards into the warmth of the mid-summer morning.

Whereas at the dawn of the day the decks, alleyways and lounges had been devoid of human activity, now they were subjected to the steady comings and goings of both crew and passengers. After the breakfast tables had been cleared the stewards busied themselves with hoovers, furniture polish and dusters. They pounded the alleyway carpets, leathered the internal window surfaces and moved from cabin to cabin adding further lustre to seemingly immaculate furniture and fittings. Though this was part and parcel of their everyday routine, Sunday was of special importance.

Traditionally, through the merchant service, Sunday morning is the occasion of the Captain's weekly inspection. I don't suppose the procedure on U.B.C. ships varies greatly to that on any other line. Accompanied by his Chief and Catering Officers, the Captain starts at the topmost deck and inspects the entire accommodation area. Checking each and every cabin, mess room, lounge, broom cupboard, alleyway and fire point, the Master makes comment to his subordinates who list the items that have met with his disapproval.

Rounding Sweden's southernmost limit, our course became more easterly and the sun poured down on the starboard side. Consequently out came the deck chairs and out came my travelling companions. The sea state was flat calm — no waves, just a progression of silver-crested ripples. While musing at the distant coastline over to port I was joined by Second Engineer John Gunning. Commenting on my remarks about the excellent weather conditions on the outward journey John Gunning sensed that a change was imminent. Whether he had heard a local forecast or was relying on instinct I do not know. What I did discover Gunning was something of an authority on climatic conditions in Baltic waters.

John Gunning, thirty-five and single, was a soft-spoken East Anglian. He was a man who not only derived a living from the sea but filled his leisure time with maritime interests. During his career he had become a keen photographer and built up a unique collection of seascape colour slides. Also, as a member of the World Ship Society, he had written short articles covering East Anglian ports and trades. Though he had joined U.B.C. two years previously and crewed 'Baltic Enterprise' for barely eighteen months one could sense his genuine affinity with the ship. Not that he had singled out 'Enterprise' as a special love in his life. I felt that his references of 'old girl' could be attached to any ship on which he served. Gunning wasn't aboard purely as a means to making a living; he was there because he liked the life. At that time he had recently taken time off to sit for his Chief Engineer's ticket. I later found out he had been successful.

The off-watch Second Engineer and I ambled along the green decks until we arrived at the open bridgehouse door. Here, with the ship now in more open water and steering on automatic pilot, we found William Maclaughlan alone on watch.

"All alone I see, young Willie." John Gunning's Norfolk accent broke the bridgehouse quiet and brought the Scotsman away from a radar console.

"Ay. I reckon the Old Man will be on his inspection by now," Maclaughlan greeted his fellow officer with spontaneous shipboard cross-talk.

"George is out there though." He indicated through the forward windows at George Hall perched on the high platform of the weather deck gantry apparently working on an electrical circuit. "I don't know if I am supposed to keep an eye on him or if he is there to spy on me!"

"What's our ETA at Helsinki?" my companion enquired.

"If we keep this pace up it's got to be early tomorrow afternoon."

The young Third Officer led us over to the chart table where he busied himself with dividers.

"I make it 14.00 at Harmarja Pilot Station so that sounds like 15.00 on-the-berth our time."

The chart showed the Swedish coast was then five miles distant. The townships visible through binoculars on this reach were clearly indicated. Trelleborg we had long passed, while over the port bow lay Ystad. This, the guide books claim, is a medieval city with narrow winding streets with hundreds of half-timbered houses. Several seaside villages were scattered along the twenty-mile shore road that linked the two towns.

Maclaughlan showed me the course we were taking across the chart. We were about to start a haul of two hundred and fifty miles on a heading of 060. This heading would shortly carry us past the Danish island of Bornholm and ultimately to the mid-Baltic east of the largest of its islands — Gotland. At that time we were almost seven hundred miles and forty hours of sailing out of Hull.

The face of Bornholm's northern cliffs showed up through the glasses right on the call for Sunday lunch. However I held on for a few minutes to gain a four-mile onshore impression of the island. Bornholm is one of Denmark's great assets. It is a popular holiday venue for thousands of Scandinavians who know it as the 'Baltic Hideaway.' Its gently rolling countryside is scattered with tiny farmsteads and round churches. Denmark possesses little mineral wealth but Bornholm has massive granite deposits. The solid grey rock of the northern part of its seventy-mile shoreline bore substantial evidence to this claim.

During my brief ground work on the island's history, I discovered that there had been many invasions, the most recent being the German occupation during the Second World War. In August 1943 the first V-1 rocket ever to land on non-German soil plunged into a Bornholm field. A young Danish policeman, Johannes Hansen, sketched and photographed this object, carefully appraising its potential. In later years this daring man was promoted to Chief of the island's Police. Rhonne is the name of Bornholm's capital. Situated on the west coast it has a population of 15,000.

When the situation allowed it, siestas were a small luxury 'Enterprise's' officers enjoyed. That is to say should the ship be at sea in fair weather the men who were off-duty would manage to squeeze a couple of hours of early afternoon relaxation. Up to the time afternoon tea was served the saloon would empty and cabin doors would close on hushed alleyways. There was a kind of reverence about that period of the day that the passengers respected.

It was not the ideal opportunity for seeking the Catering Officer to purchase cigarettes, chocolates or spirits. Nor was it the time to be looking for the Captain or Chief Officer to ask questions of no immediate importance. If out and about during this period of the day one would surreptitiously tread the alleyways more lightly, voices would be toned down and cabin doors would be closed with a greater degree of care.

With Sunday lunch consumed and the tables cleared, people disappearing to quiet corners of the accommodation and, outdoors, Bornholm Island fading into a hazy image on the distant horizon, I duly retired to catch up with my notes. Within the hour, as I sat at a desk littered with papers, tape recordings, chart sections and the like, there was a cautious knock at my cabin door. Following two days of probing around with note book and pencil, my attentive quest had been accepted by the crew and had germinated among the passengers.

Bob Turnbull had been keeping Bernard Elworthy company on his 12.00 — 16.00 stint on the bridge. The young Second Officer had suspected that we would soon be within sight of the largest and fastest ferry ship afloat. Bob Turnbull, as enthusiastic as I was, could not wait to volunteer this information.

During the early seventies, Oy Finnlines, of Helsinki, evaluated the long-term potential of Baltic passenger traffic. After much detailed project work the idea of using one super ferry instead of three ordinary vessels evolved. Subsequently an order was placed and in 1977 'Finnjet,' 23,000 gross tons, entered service on the Helsinki — Travemunde, West Germany route. Operating at an incredible $30\frac{1}{2}$ knots, this huge ship is capable of completing the 1,300-mile round voyage in two days. On inauguration not only did 'Finnjet' become the largest and fastest but was to be the first gas turbine passenger ferry in the world.

On noticing a rapidly advancing 'blip' on our long-range radar, Elworthy had kept more than the normal routine interest. This large response was eating its way across the range rings at nearly twice the normal pace. His instinct told him that this could only be one ship.

The three of us stood on the bridge wing as, on a reciprocal bearing, 'Finnjet' stormed rapidly towards us out of the afternoon heat haze several points over to port. As the closing speed between our burdened ro-ro and this spectacular giant ferry was somewhere in the order of 50 knots, it was but a smattering of brief minutes before we were in close contact.

'Finnjet' appeared to be something of a cruise liner, bulk carrier and destroyer all rolled into one. Having cabin accommodation for 1,532 passengers her gleaming white superstructure gave the multi-windowed look of a sea-edge hotel. Beneath, witnessed with 'Finnjet' in oversized white lettering amidships, her capacious hull was in the league of the ocean greats. Despite this vastness she was rolling a bow-wave of convulsed Baltic water with all the fury of a hard-pressed warship. Abeam of us her twin-raked funnels, bearing the motif 'F,' issued a blur of hot grey smoke. This was quickly left hanging high above the foaming tumult she emitted astern. 'Finnjet' was being powered along by two Pratt and Whitney gas turbines each developing 37,500 horsepower. To maintain her extremely tight sailing schedule the two propulsion units were installed as totally independent units. Should one unit fail, the ship has the ability to maintain 24 knots on the other.

All passengers are housed in cabins which are well forward to minimise noise and vibration. The public rooms are located aft separated from the cabin areas by large lobbies. Together with the usual restaurants and bars, these amenities include a night club, disco, shopping centre, swimming pool, sauna and gymnasium.

"In heavy weather I have seen her completely shrouded in sea-spray," Elworthy commented while his two passengers marvelled at the passing ship.

"She hardly ever seems to slow regardless of the sea state. Huge oncoming waves are smashed by that high-raked bow. Festoons of opaque water are thrust skywards — higher and over her entire superstructure."

I must confess that when younger I found the conflicting arrangements of measuring ships something of a mystery. In this respect I was no freak of nature for the landsman often refers to a vessel as being of so many tons without really understanding the meaning of tonnage as applied to ships. It was not until my interest in shipping proliferated had I any idea of how the system was applied. Here my investigations revealed that normally passenger and general cargo ships are expressed in gross tons. Tankers and bulk carriers are recorded by deadweight tonnage while displacement tonnage is usually related to warships.

Gross tonnage is a measurement of volume not weight. Calculated at 100 cubic feet to the ton, the gross tonnage is the total cubic capacity of all the permanently enclosed space — that is both hull and superstructure together.

Deadweight tonnage is the actual weight in tons of cargo, stores, fuel and ballast that a ship is capable of carrying when submerged to her load line.

Displacement tonnage, on the other hand, is the total weight of the ship and its contents. Equally this is the number of tons of water displaced by the vessel when floating at her load line.

Throughout I have adhered to this when indicating the tonnage of a ship. However, purely to illustrate how this variety of measurements could misconstrue one's evaluation of a ship, I would mention that although 'Baltic Enterprise' was registered at 4,667 gross tons, her deadweight tonnage was 5,600 and her displacement was over 12,000 tons. As a marked contrast the 12,988 gross ton Hull registered ferry 'Norland' has a deadweight tonnage of only 3,800.

Seeing 'Finnjet' ploughing through the Baltic that day had been an unexpected bonus, moreover when, soon afterwards, there was a marked deterioration in visibility. Around Bornholm the horizon had become decidedly indistinct. From then on we had been sailing into a murky sea-level haze yet still overlooked by an immaculate sky of blue. But now the curtain had grown thicker and higher, blotting out the sun and leaving us pounding north-eastwards trammelled within a two-mile radius world of drab sea mist.

Suddenly the Baltic was a less attractive place to be in. Its sparkling silver-blue hue had transformed into a ponderous grey wash. Being essentially an inland sea, the Baltic is sometimes called the 'Mediterranean of the North.' Like this denizen of the south, many races and cultures meet round its shores.

In the Middle Ages the Hanseatic League was an alliance of trading towns fronting the Baltic. This was governed from the German town of Lubeck. Though large industrial centres have grown and flourished there since those times, so have political frontiers. Indeed the very trade upon which the United Baltic Corporation was founded is now secured behind the Iron Curtain.

To begin with the U.B.C. house flag was first shown around the Baltic in the summer of 1919. At the end of the First World War passenger and cargo services between Britain and the Baltic States were so disorganised that many potentially important shipping centres of the eastern seaboard had no direct links with London. To meet this situation the United Baltic Corporation was launched by way of a joint agreement between Andrew Weir & Co. Ltd., of London, and the East Asiatic Company of Copenhagen, the Danish side of this union already having interests in the Baltic through its subsidiary the Russian East Asiatic Steamship Company.

Initially the Corporation had no ships, so short-term charters were arranged for four of the East Asiatic ships. Within twelve months three of these vessels had been purchased by U.B.C. and renamed 'Baltriger,' 'Baltannic' and 'Baltabor.' Each of these ships was in the region of 1,200 gross tons, the former two having accommodation for up to 130 passengers. In these early days Danzig (now Gdansk) in Poland and ports in the East Baltic States of Latvia, Lithuania and Estonia were serviced. In the between war years, trade bloomed and the Corporation progressively improved its fleet by successive purchases of more adaptable and capacious ships. All ships used the Kiel Canal and branch offices and agencies were opened up on regular routes. From the outset passengers were carried on all routes. In 1923 special holiday trips were advertised in connection with summer sailings to the Baltic. These remained popular and in the late thirties the minimum rate for a voyage of twelve days was twelve guineas. With the introduction of the Corporation's first 'Baltrover' (4,916 gross tons) in 1935 nearly 200 passengers could be carried on every Danzig-Gdynia sailing. About this time U.B.C. ships carried hundreds of Jewish emigrants from Lithuania and Latvia to London en route for North and South America.

Baltic sailings were suspended in September 1939, and the fleet, under Admiralty and Ministry of War Transport direction, saw service in all parts of the world. Four U.B.C. vessels were lost through mines or torpedoes.

As soon as normal trading conditions returned, Polish services were reopened from both London and Hull but the other regular Baltic State sailings could not be resumed. The Corporation looked in other directions and the current U.K./Finland services were inaugurated. The Hull/Leningrad route was added in 1959. The early 50's saw a change in naming policy. From then onwards each ship was prefixed 'Baltic.' The first to come under this change were the 1,900 gross tons sister ships 'Baltic Fir,' 'Pine' and 'Oak.'

Today the general decline in world trade and shipping together with the advent of ro-ro systems has left its mark on the Corporation's fleet list. Yet operating three ro-ro vessels and two conventional general cargo ships, U.B.C. continues to service the Baltic through the routes to Gdynia and Leningrad along with the heavy involvement in the Finnanglia operation.

CHAPTER SEVEN

Gone Monday noontime we were still pushing north-east on a heading of 060 degrees but now crossing the eastern arm of the Baltic Sea known as the Gulf of Finland. With more than one thousand sea miles behind us we were within three hours of the Helsinki waterfront.

Unfortunately John Gunning's prediction of Sunday morning had been more than accurate. The almost perfect weather conditions that we had enjoyed during the 'lion's share' of the voyage from Hull had disappeared behind an oppressive blanket of sea fog. As if the total loss of visibility was not enough the elements had decided to treat us to frequent heavy showers that lashed at the ship's forward-facing windows and puddled her decks throughout the morning.

The sea, grey, dull and uneasy, prompted 'Baltic Enterprise' into a motion that could not be characterised as either pitching or rolling. Time and again she would begin to dip her bow towards the troughs of oncoming seas only to change her attitude to the situation before becoming fully committed. This abandonment would lead into a short sequence of lateral restlessness that sometimes was enough to effect facial reactions of unsteady passengers but went almost un-noticed among the crew. Up forward, adding to the precipitation, sea-spray was regularly thrust skywards up and over the tops of weather deck cargo. These saturating bouts were continuously induced through conflicting efforts of ruffled seas upon the ship's undaunted forward progress.

Conforming with regulations, Gerry Brazendale had been on his bridge ever since the fog closed in. This uncompassionate turn of events, though intimidating from Sunday lunchtime, had transpired some two hundred miles back. Brazendale's vigil was now in its thirteenth hour. Fog or no fog, not once had our speed been reduced. Guided entirely on her navigational aids, 'Enterprise' had surged through the Baltic at 'ten ahead' holding her expected schedule almost to the minute. It was not a cold day. Yet in protest to the dank realism outdoors high-necked navy blue pullovers were the uniform for the occasion. Contrasting with the youthful stature of the Second Officer, Brazendale's new garb, opulently displaying four gold braid bars at each shoulder, disclosed his portly advancement towards middle age. Through hours of peering down at the orange glowing radar consoles his eyes were beginning to bear signs of tiredness. So too, on uprighting himself away from the screens, was the habitual removal of flopping hair from his broad forehead. His drooping fringe was a form of styling that began to irritate the situation rather than help it.

This was by no means the first time Brazendale had guided a ship towards the outlying islands of Finland through adverse weather; neither would it be his last. Nevertheless it was not an assignment a master would savour. Unrelenting he had paced between the main facia and the chart table checking and counter-checking the information fed by the radar and Decca Navigator. Infrequently, while on these seemingly automatic excursions across the bridgehouse carpet, he would bisect the path of his watch-keeping officer. The encounter would induce a brief flurry of conversation that rarely deviated from the job in hand. All three deck officers had stood watch through his long vigil. Each respected his wish to sidestep any other subject. Other than the sounds from the ship's instrumentation the only respite from long spells of silence was offered every two minutes by the fog siren way out on the mist-encircled fore-mast.

Barely thirty-five sea miles separated us from Harmarja. From this island base, the pilot would effect a rendezvous and accompany us along the remaining three miles of tightly buoyed water. Racing towards that point obscured from the outside world I sensed that the last flicker of relaxation had been extinguished. Making my presence in the bridgehouse as diminutive as possible, I found a remote corner and whiled away several advancing miles thumbing through my notes of that morning.

From breakfast onwards the accommodation block had been thronged with more activity than at any previous time. With our impending landfall effecting the departure of the Jackson family, and a more than refreshed transport driver, suitcases were to be seen outside cabin doors. Road maps of Finland were spread out on the lounge tables. Accounts were being settled and 'duty frees' collected at the catering office.

Irrespective of the inclement outdoor scene, my morning had been utilised to full advantage. Following up an invitation to see the mechanical side of the ship, 09.30 saw me donning a pair of sound-proofed ear protectors in the office of Chief Engineer, Clive Buchan. With more than twenty-five years service with U.B.C., Buchan was one of the company's more senior engineers. Tyneside has an age-long tradition of producing first-class marine engineers — Clive Buchan was born and bred there — his soft Geordie accent clearly backing this claim. I have always had a good rapport with Tynesiders; this association was no exception.

Our journey to the engine room commenced at a door that hinged from the port-side alleyway on the boat deck. Wearing a grease-stained white boiler-suit the Chief led the way onto the first of seven flights of steel stairs that progressively criss-crossed down a brilliantly lit shaft. At first we seemed to be encompassed within a strong updraught of hot air. However, after dropping three levels, the main impact came from hard-working machinery. Regardless of firmly positioned ear muffs the almighty commotion emitted from below became implanted in each nerve and muscle — it gripped every breath of air. Buchan had made the descent a thousand times. For him the dramatic and sudden change from the comparable hush of the living area to this erupting cauldron of noise was of no more consequence than the switching on of a radio.

Mine was a descent filled with intrigue and caution to the extent that Clive Buchan was looking quizzically upwards when I arrived at the last landing. Putting noise aside the next captivating element was the generous amount of light afforded. Together with the many ranks of strip lights, liberal use of white, cream and light-blue gloss paint gave the engine room an almost clinical effect. Down at base level, one felt to be centred in a floodlit arena packed to capacity with all manner of pulsating machinery. After threading along grey painted steel walkways flanked by pipes and cables of varying sizes, heat and energy, seething auxiliary mechanisms and overhead warning notices we reached a tightly closed door.

Conversation had been out of the question but following my companion's sign language I was quickly guided inside a soundproofed haven. Seated there, at a bank of multi-dialled consoles, was Scotsman Bob Cairns. Together with Paul Davey, Cairns carried the rank of Third Engineer. As we were not carrying a 'Fourth,' Cairns had stepped into that watch stint. With all its futuristic animation, air conditioning and sound protection, the control room was a place of sanctuary. There the engineers settle after an initial on-watch half-hour tour of routine checks and adjustments.

The Chief explained his watch-keeper's responsibilities through monitoring the data displayed. "It is vital that any trouble should be spotted and remedial action taken straight away."

Some of the control room instrumentation was a duplicate of that seen on the bridge. Chiefly this included dials and gauges giving performance readings of the main engines. Relevant levers offered an alternative engine control position should the bridge system fail. Apart from the obvious importance of propulsion units and generators, a ship relies upon a host of auxiliary systems to keep it functional. An assembly of lights that gave warning of faults within such areas was a prominent feature of the main facia.

With talk of ventilators, compressed air starters, fuel heaters and water supply pressurisation we were only scratching the surface. From then on I realised that to explain the ship's mechanical make-up would require more pages than in this book and, moreover, someone more qualified than myself to scribe them.

Leaving Bob Cairns to his coloured lights, advancing digits, twitching dials and data-filled log books, the Chief led me back stage. Within this unmanned ante-room were sited three substantial diesel-powered generators that were capable of lighting several streets of houses.

"Electricity is the very life-blood of the ship. Without it almost every single mechanical function — from windlasses to windscreen wipers, radar to refrigerators, direction finder to domestic services — would grind to an eerie silence."

Clive Buchan indicated that only one of the diesels was running. "When we dock, later in the day, all three 'gennys' will be called for. It's the cranes, lifts and deck gear that make the meter race round — I hope you have some 10p pieces ready!"

Facing the line-up of generators was a bank of shining grey consoles. They housed a complex of intricate switchgear that was linked to the miles of wiring threaded around the ship.

In the days of sail a ship's engineers were the carpenter and the sailmaker. Through their individual skills and versatility in the art of improvisation, ships that were theoretically doomed often limped to safety.

A section of the engine room.

Erecting make-shift masts, repairing smashed steering gear and resurrecting shredded sails with ten thousand stitches was their line of business.

Timber and canvas are not commodities easily found aboard a modern ship. Consequently the engineer's workshop is equipped to fashion steel. Lathes, drills, grinders and vices were the principal furnishings in this section of the engine room complex aboard 'Baltic Enterprise.' Though the ship carried a comprehensive store of mechanical parts, the engineers had to be resourceful. Spread around steel-topped work benches was a wide variety of oil-clad components. They had been replaced as worn out, faulty or were just in need of servicing. "Costly parts can't be written off at random. If we can repair them on the spot we do so — otherwise they are sent to marine workshops ashore. The majority of the work carried out in this workshop is routine servicing, which is one continuous process."

Buchan added: "So you can see there is more to this job than sitting in the control room."

"These ships are driven hard to maintain schedules unthinkable two decades ago. There's no time in port worthy of mention to carry out general repairs. Only a major breakdown distorts the schedule. Even then contingency plans are put into operation. We have to put to sea on one engine with engineers working on the defective one. Naturally the weather holds the key to the progress we make under half power. In favourable conditions we have maintained twelve knots or more."

'Enterprise's' propulsion units were two Stork-Werkspoor 9TM410 diesels each developing 5,250 b.h.p. at 530 r.p.m. To anyone other than those directly connected with marine engineering this information means little. However if I were to mention that each of these engines weighed eighty-five metric tons, measured twenty-five feet in length and stood some eleven feet in height, the layman should begin to appreciate their size. As a comparison, they would simply dwarf a juggernaut lorry engine into looking as though it belonged to a matchbox toy.

From the workshop I followed Clive Buchan onto an elevated catwalk that ran forward the full length of the starboard engine. Diesel engines consume oxygen in limitless quantities. Sited well below the waterline, those of a ship can only be fed from above. Four powerful ventilators were blending a strong down-current of Baltic sea-tanged air with a hot, oil-tainted ozone. Amid this swirling mistral we paused. Both these nine-in-line engines were turning over at 510 r.p.m. — medium speed diesels in marine terms. Through gearing they were revolving fifteen-inch diameter propeller shafts at 200 r.p.m. Standing at the rail with the nine cylinder heads at knee high, the noise was beyond description. With ear protectors the impression was of the roar at the base of a mighty waterfall. Without them — momentarily I eased the muffs away from my head — the convulsed air reverberated within the grip of a dynamic scream that bludgeoned the ear drums way beyond the limit of my expectations.

Together, running as they were, these rasping monsters consumed thirty tons of fuel oil every twenty-four hours. Though this seemed a colossal amount, I was assured it was no greater than expected of a ship with an output in excess of ten thousand horsepower.

On returning heavenwards to the sanity of the officers' mess, Clive Buchan poured out mid-morning coffee. At this time of day off-watch officers drifted through the portal of their boat-deck retreat. The occasion was known aboard as Smoko — a fifteen minute break where, amid the airing of views over topical issues, tea and coffee of their own brewing flowed from seemingly bottomless pots. Among the now familiar faces of Messrs Green, Hall, Elworthy, Garvey, Davey and Gunning, I began to collect my thoughts over the engine room visit. Questions that I had been unable to ask through the unholy racket down there were now answered.

My presence did not interrupt their social exchange — those not involved in engineering talk overlooked my occupancy of the port-side

91

table. Neither did my being there overshadow a report to the Chief from Davey and Gunning on the work they had carried out below decks. Apparently, while at Hull, there had been some mechanical trouble with one of the two cargo lifts on the lower 'tween deck. Over the past two days each of these men had spent several hours stripping part of a hydraulic system to replace worn seals; the lift had to be serviceable for the turn-round at Helsinki.

"I'll come down at eleven and we'll give her a final work-out," was Clive Buchan's reply to their confirmation of 'job completed.' "As you can see an engineer's lot does not start and finish in the engine room alone. Whether it be winches, stern doors, cranes or lifts they all need attention at some time or other. With the ship being at sea most of its life that is when the work is carried out. We have strict maintenance schedules to which, if at all practically possible, we adhere regardless of the position of the ship."

Soon after eleven I made my way across a rain-soaked after-deck to join the party of engineers below. Retracing my route from whence I first came aboard, I descended three stairways to find myself within the ship's cavernous belly. It was a gaunt lifeless place. Walls of steel, deck of steel, roof of steel and, not the least, more solid than a house side, two towering dungeon doors rammed square across the stern. Aftermost a cold track-marked deck shook involuntarily at the thrusting of the screws directly below. This vibration rang through the wide tunnel of the 'tween deck. Augmented with a ceaseless roar from the nearby engines, it set up an undying metallic thunder that equalled any severe bashing of an empty drum. Yet this cargo hold was far from empty. Lanes of low-load trailers bearing either secretly sealed containers or inanimate shapes of a miscellany of British-made machinery were lashed downwards with bar-tight chains.

In a clearing midst this sleeping freight, I watched Buchan work at push-button controls. A thirteen-metre section of the deck steadily sank to the depths of the lower hold. With me at the surrounding guard rail seeing the lift platform faultlessly sink to the deck below were a somewhat contented Gunning and Davey.

The process of taking the forty-five ton lift to its travel limits was repeated several times. Eventually Buchan, satisfied that the system was functioning correctly, came over to compliment his engineers. In doing so he asked Gunning to make a final check when the lift was operating under loaded conditions at Helsinki.

My morning spent touring the ship's innards was concluded by a brief look at the rudder mechanism. Following Paul Davey down a vertical ladder sited somewhere near the stern doors, I entered a deep-seated compartment where one could hardly stand upright. Much of this claustro-phobic place was filled by the vertical mandrel on which the rudder pivoted and the hefty arms that activated this movement. Davey was there to carry out a routine inspection. In doing so he wasted no time. Here again the noise level was explosive — away from the main engines it must have rated as one of the noisiest areas aboard ship, not a place to linger, particularly when, several decks above, the smoke-room bar had opened for lunchtime beverages.

Settled in the port corner of the bridgehouse, I gazed aimlessly out over a rain and spray-drenched weather deck into an everlasting fog. Though the two navigators stationed there knew our exact position relative to the Finnish capital, for all I could see we could have just as well been nearing New York, Sydney or Hong Kong. It was not a time for questions so I quietly penned down the bridgehouse activity until we berthed mid-afternoon at Helsinki West Harbour. Extracts from my notes read thus:

12.45 Bridge manned by Captain and Second Officer. Course — 060. Speed — 18½ knots. Distance to Helsinki pilot — 20 miles. Visibility — approx. 200 yards. Rain has ceased. Ship on auto pilot. Rolling steadily.
Brazendale in subdued mood finishing tray lunch that has been placed on drop-leaf table at the starboard bulkhead. Elworthy peering deeply into port-side radar console. Two of the three radar sets are fitted with daylight masks.

12.50 Radio Officer Roy Caple enters through inner door bearing message which he takes to Brazendale at chart table. Similarly steward enters with coffee tray for the two men on watch. He quietly stacks remnants of Brazendale's lunch and within a matter of seconds is gone.

13.00 Visibility slightly improved. Brazendale dons peaked hat, slides back starboard door and scours binoculars into mist from bridge wing. Shortly he returns to radar screen. (Obviously there are other ships close at hand responding to our radar beams but not physically in view.)

13.10 Visibility back to 200 yards. Brazendale sips coffee that by now must be cold. Arranged rendezvous with pilot — 14.00. Elworthy rings Bo'sun to have flags hoisted. Shortly A.B. arrives at starboard wing door — Elworthy hands him Red Ensign, U.B.C. house flag and Finnish courtesy flag.

13.20 Clive Buchan arrives on bridge — checks engine revs., speed through water and then stands at side of Master who is yet again at radar screen. Fog is now dense and rain sheeting down. Ship still rolling gently. Buchan holds short conversation with Brazendale then picks up spare binoculars and scans into fog that is almost engulfing our bow.

13.25 Elworthy at chart table calls over to Brazendale informing him that we have reached position to change course. Captain adjusts auto-pilot to effect 15 degree port turn. Now on 045. Fog eases considerably. We sight small freighter approx. 150 yards to starboard. This ship is also heading for Helsinki but due to our much superior speed it is soon overhauled.

13.30   Distance to pilot — 7 miles. Distance to Helsinki — 10 miles. Speed — 18½ knots. Course — 045. Rain has stopped and sky is brighter than at any other time today. Fog continues but clear patches becoming more frequent. Fog siren still issuing two-minutely announcements from its fore-mast perch.

13.40   Brazendale asks Elworthy for a helmsman. Elworthy rings Bo'sun for an A.B. and advises him that the pilot boat will come along port side.

13.43   Helmsman arrives — makes careful study of compass display and asks if he has to hold 045.
Brazendale: "Easy to port!"
Though there is no skyline on which to follow this steady swing one can physically feel the ship pulling round onto a more northerly heading.
Brazendale: "Midships! Steady!"
Helmsman: "Steady 005, sir!"

13.50   Fog is very thick. Brazendale moves constantly between the three radar displays, then turns to Elworthy: "Give pilots a call please."
Elworthy responds: "Baltic Enterprise — Harmarja pilot — we shall be at your station in ten minutes."
Reply over V.H.F. loudspeaker: "Thank you, Baltic Enterprise — understand ten minutes."

13.55   Fog very thick. Brazendale brings engines down from 10 to 5 ahead. Briefly looks at radar then returns to controls and brings engines down to 2 ahead. Now muted and enclosed within thick blanket of sea fog, ship ambles lethargically forward at will of grey cross swell.

14.00   Brazendale and Elworthy constantly scanning for pilot boat both through radar and binoculars.
Brazendale: "How does she head?"
Helmsman: "003, sir."
No sign of pilot boat. Brazendale takes chart over to table near radar screen.

14.03   Gulls loom over weather deck as though to guide us through fog — fog siren booms out and they hasten away.
Brazendale: "005!"
Helmsman: "005."
Progress — dead slow.

14.05   Red and white beacon appears close down starbord side, another shows up to port. Rocky islet topped with lighthouse looms out of mist few points to port. This is Harmarja!
Brazendale: "007!"
Helmsman: "007."
Brazendale: "Have you got someone standing by for the pilot?"
Elworthy: "Yes, sir."

14.06   Pilot launch painted cream and red powers out the of mist on port side.

Making for our pilot door it livens up the grey water with a half-circle of foaming wake. Brazendale asks Elworthy to go down to the weather deck to meet pilot. Elworthy leaves by internal door.

14.07 Launch alongside — dwarfed by our ship's towering hull. Pilot climbs rope ladder and is helped through door. Visibility improves considerably — long string of islands beyond Harmarja now in view.

Brazendale from port wing: "015!"

Helmsman: "015."

Entering bridgehouse Brazendale opens engine controls to 5 ahead both.

14.09 Elworthy and pilot enter bridgehouse. Brazendale greets pilot with customary hand-shake. He is a fair-haired man of medium build donned in waterproofs. Walking to bridgehouse he calls to helmsman: "Port easy . . . midships . . . steady!" His English is surprisingly clear. For the first time in several hours the pressure is momentarily off the Captain — he walks over to me and comments on the irony of the climatic conditions: "Incredible isn't it; as soon as the pilot steps aboard that damned fog leaves us; should have picked him up two hundred miles back!"

14.10 Now abeam of Harmarja Island — apart from lighthouse can see number of low buildings on rocky site — this is the pilot station. Fog has cleared — hazy sunshine breaking through. Helsinki waterfront, distance — 3 miles, appears on skyline between nearby islands.

14.12 Elworthy on internal phone informs first and third officers that we shall be docking in 15 minutes.

Pilot: "Port ten!"

Helmsman: "Port ten."

Brazendale now uncovering engine controls on port wing.

Recognisable on our starboard side was Suomenlinna, this being an eighteenth century sea fortress that links a group of five islands. What a splendid entry to Finland Suomenlinna makes — its rugged stone ramparts rear from grassy knolls and granite shores to guard the entrance to Helsinki's South Harbour. The fortress was built under Swedish rule and was called Sveaborg (Sweden Fort). On completion it was considered to be impregnable but, haplessly, was belittled by the bombardment of Anglo-French forces in 1855 during the Crimean War.

I well remember seeing, on the television series 'Royal Heritage,' film of the Queen's arrival at Helsinki during her summer visit of 1976. The Royal Yacht 'Britannia' sailed alongside Suomenlinna's eastern shores. Here, bathed in brilliant sunshine, ranks of military guards were stood to attention. From the after decks of their ship, Her Majesty and Prince Philip acknowledged a salute fired from cannons at the fortress walls. The Royal Yacht berthed at South Harbour, this being a fitting location to conduct

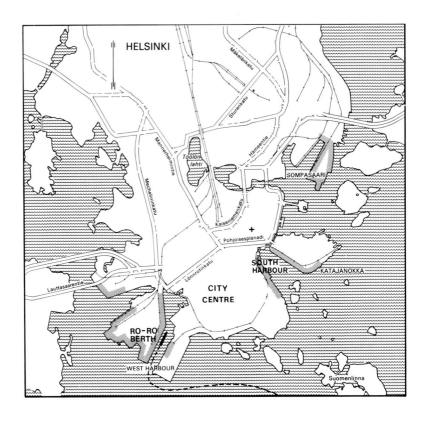

such a visit. I feel certain that it was an occasion that the Royal Couple will long remember.

Through the dramatic change in the weather our arrival at Helsinki exceeded all expectations. Our destination was to be the commercial docks of the West Harbour, so the pilot guided the ship past the south-west shores of Suomenlinna. Here and there its grassy slopes were dotted with families taking an afternoon vacation from the city. Pacing nearer to the terminal a grey and white ribbon of majestic buildings freshened by the departed rain spread across our northern seaboard. Set some distance back from the waterfront but crowning this elegant facade was the green-domed tower of Helsinki's Lutheran Cathedral. It is often said that Helsinki should be first seen from the sea, preferably in the summertime. I was fortunate enough to fall into such an introduction.

14.15 Suomenlinna to starboard — pilot calling course changes intermittently — "Port ten — five — five."
Bo'sun and crewmen work on crane releases then walk out to

the forward mooring deck. Green replaces Elworthy on bridge.

14.18   Wooded island to port — Helsinki waterfront directly to starboard. Making for industrial complex — cranes, sheds and quays. Maclaughlan and two crewmen on aft mooring deck. Pilot following buoyed channel weaves ship tightly first to starboard then to port.

14.20   Brazendale at engine controls. Speed approx. 7 knots. Now only half a mile off shore.

14.23   Factory complex on peninsula of land directly to starboard. Pilot edges ship round this promontory through constant calls to helmsman — "Starboard twenty! Hard to starboard! Midships! Hard to starboard! Midships!"

The nucleus of Helsinki is sited on a peninsula of land that spreads itself seawards in a most irregular fashion. Really it would be best described as an island situation with numerous jig-saw-like off-shoots reaching from its central hub — the northern arm being the link with the mainland. Needless to say one does not have to walk far from the centre before being confronted by water. West Harbour (Lansisatama) is an inroad stretching the best part of a mile between what appeared to be reclaimed fingers of land.

The pilot's tight starboard turn of ninety degrees had brought our ship into the West Harbour and faced her towards the City itself. Within this cul-de-sac she was eased at less than walking pace towards a clearing between a string of ships at the quay some six hundred yards from the main waterfront. Brazendale, operating from the port wing, was now very much back in command. Using the same dexterity over the engine controls that he had demonstrated three days earlier in the confines at Hull, he glided 'Enterprise' to a standstill angled some twenty degrees to the vacant quay.

All at once, after more than a thousand miles of open water, the world closed in on us. We were among lines of sheds and cranes, there were ships both ahead and astern, over on the opposite bank our starboard side faced factories displaying the names of 'Ford' and 'Volvo.' Ahead the rain-soaked rooftops of the City dried under an ever-strengthening sun.

At our arrival the quayside seemed to burst into life. Cars and people busied between the buildings and offices. Shore crews at the water's edge looked skywards awaiting our warps. Tractors with flashing lights atop of their cabs were rev-ing in readiness for the assault on our cargo. Officials with clipboards stood by for the moment they could be aboard.

Beneath our stern a broad concrete ramp reached from the main frontage for more than a ship's breadth. Bo'sun Edwards and his men, reacting swiftly to a command from their captain, occupied themselves with our forward lines — ultimately it was against these warps that Brazendale worked his engines to swing 'Enterprise' nearer the quay and face her huge doors at the ramp. Through an Olympic class throw a member of our after-deck crew had the 'monkey's fist' end of his heaving-line scurrying over the concrete more than twenty feet below. From then on, apart from a few final adjustments by both winches and engines, we were as good as berthed.

As Brazendale rested the control levers of his ever-willing engines into the zero position, Bernard Elworthy, now stationed on the after-deck, had both stern doors hingeing from the vertical. Simultaneously, Peter Green, at the chart table desk, busied himself with the ship's log. His entry was concluding another short chapter in an encyclopedia of voyages.

Glancing at his wrist watch while gratefully relaxing his frame against the white rail of the wing, Gerry Brazendale called to his Chief Officer: "Sixty-seven hours to the minute!"

I doubt whether Green heard the Captain voice his satisfaction for there was no reply. As it was, he already knew that we had made good time. The ship's chronometer before him read 14.30 precisely.

CHAPTER EIGHT

Helsinki has not always been the capital of Finland. Nor have the Finns always enjoyed autonomous government. Indeed in terms of independence Finland is a relatively young country. Under many centuries of Swedish rule, Turku, a hundred miles or so to the west, was deemed to be favourably close to Stockholm and thus ideally situated to be the Finnish capital.

At the beginning of the 19th century, under ever-increasing pressure from the east, the Swedish realm was at a low ebb. There had been many wars between Sweden and Russia on Finnish soil through which the Finns gained little and lost much. In 1809 Finland was ceded to Russia and a new epoch began. As a Grand Duchy of Russia the seat of government was established at Helsinki. This was 1812 when the town had a population of only four thousand. However, Tsar Alexander I commanded that Helsinki should be rebuilt in accordance with its new status of capital. From an extensive construction programme, largely executed by a native of Helsinki, J. A. Ehrenstrom, and the German-born architect C. L. Engel, a city of great dignity evolved. Commanding the northern flank of Senate Square (Engel's most impressive contribution) Helsinki Cathedral highlights the classical style of this period.

Exactly one hundred years later the Grand Duchy was dissolved and Finland became part and parcel of the Russian Empire. It was not until the Russian revolution in March 1917 that the ultimate ideal of independence came within the grasp of the Finnish people. During this time of political upheaval they brought pressure to bear and returned to exercise powers belonging to the days of the Tsar. The Russian government of the day raised no objection and on 6th December 1917 Finland proudly declared her independence.

Originally founded under Swedish rule in 1550, Helsinki (then Helsingfors) realised little of its anticipated commercial success for more than a century. At this stage the town was uprooted to a site near a better harbour — from then on the present Helsinki began. Even then Helsinki saw many years of difficulty — not the least having been subjected to many 'Great Fires,' this being the fate of many timber-built Finnish towns of the age. A great deal of Helsinki's early problems, however, were precipitated through the regular conflicts between Sweden and Russia.

Through this periodic sequence of rebuilding, the face of today's Helsinki is relatively modern. With a population approaching three-quarters of a million, the residential suburbs reach away from the peninsula site. Several islands have been linked to the mainland by a road system that to many brings the city centre within a fifteen-minute journey.

Being chosen as Finland's capital and premier port, Helsinki is naturally poised to accommodate ships. Its jig-saw shore-line contorts in a sequence of unregimented inroads where one can see anything from visiting cruise-liners to neat rows of motorboats.

At her West Harbour berth, 'Baltic Enterprise' was located less than two miles from the central shopping area and principal tourist attractions. But, unless for some unforeseen reason we should be delayed in port overnight, to the ship's crew Helsinki was as remote as the stars. These restrictions created by the rapid roll-on roll-off turn-round system do not apply to crewmen alone. As a round voyage passenger one has to accept whatever opportunity there may be to go ashore, no matter how brief, as a bonus to the sea voyage. In this instance our ship was to discharge 3,000 tons of cargo then take aboard approximately 1,000 tons. We would be berthed at West Harbour not an hour longer than it would take to complete this process. From the moment the stern doors had been lowered, a boisterous gang of Finnish dockworkers, our own crew-members and a variety of visiting officials had our turn-round under way. From the very off the whole ship buzzed with activity — the decks, walkways and accommodation alleyways became alien to the places we had known. It all underlined the fact that 'Enterprise' was due at her second port of call, Kotka, early next day.

"How long shall we be staying in Helsinki?" This had been a question that had been asked on more than one occasion during the outward voyage. It had been a question no-one seemed keen to provide a direct answer to.

"It all depends on how much cargo they have for us," was the most popular reply.

Finally Bob and Ruth Turnbull and myself were assured that the ship would not be sailing until some time late evening. "If this was a conventional freighter I could have promised you at least two days ashore," John Garvey said as he handed over our stamped up passports. "I recommend that you return no later than 20.30 hours ship's time," were Garvey's farewell words at his office door as the three of us made off for Finnish soil.

Down on the quay we said our goodbyes to our travelling companions. The Jacksons were packing luggage into the boot of their Cortina. Likewise Philip Rowe's removal truck had been driven ashore. We found him somewhat impatiently pacing around awaiting final clearance.

Through the foresight of John Garvey we had been offered a lift into town by a young Finn. He had been to the ship to deliver a portfolio of documents from the Helsinki agents. Our short journey in the tiny Datsun was an experience in itself. No sooner had we finished waving our goodbyes to the Jacksons than we realised that our chauffeur assumed a style in keeping with the dynasty of world-famous Finnish rally drivers. Weaving between dockland cranes, lanes of containers and a miscellany of traffic, the little car miraculously escaped what seemed inevitable. The 'rocket' take-offs, almost two-wheeled cornering and last-second braking were far removed from the smooth progress of the past three days.

There was little doubt that the uniformity of the sea journey had put us at discord with the present-day doctrine of breakneck speeds — suddenly we had moved from one extreme to the other. As, at a remarkable rate of knots, we approached the docks exit point our companion casually turned his attention away from the road and pointed in the direction of a wide basin of shimmering water. At the water's edge there were several buildings similar in appearance to aircraft hangars though considerably taller. The stern of a ship's hull was poking out from one of them.

"It is here that Finland's famous icebreakers are built," our driver proudly announced.

Not wishing to distract him any further from his driving, I did not press the young man for many details. Later, under more comfortable circumstances, I learned that the sheds form part of the giant Wartsila shipyard where apart from icebreakers the Finns build ships of all categories both for home and abroad. Very much on the 'home' front was the building of 'Finnjet' at this yard in 1976.

To this extent shipbuilding is a relatively new industry in Finland. It was not until after a considerable slice of their best forest land had been lost to Russia in 1946 that the Finns looked towards establishing resources away from the traditional woodworking industries. They decided to specialise in the heavy equipment most closely related to their own needs. Initially this meant papermaking machines and icebreakers. Such was their success that today they have cornered a large percentage of world markets for these products.

None too soon the Datsun screeched to a halt at a set of city centre traffic lights.

"This is where I leave you," we were unexpectedly advised.

So, midst the rev-ing engines of three lanes of traffic we hastily scrambled for the door. Lucklessly we were out of the frying pan into the fire for no sooner had Bob and Ruth emerged from the rear seats of the two-door car than the lights changed to green. How our visit to the Finnish capital avoided a premature ending I shall never know. Helsinki drivers are renowned for attempting to emulate their national heroes; we had just sampled this ego, and we had been marooned centrally in a melée of them. Sandwiched between two lanes of horn-rasping vehicles we stood our ground until, after what seemed an eternity, the traffic lights granted our freedom.

Within the last few minutes Ruth's healthy sun-reddened glow had changed to a sallow greenness. I parted company with the Turnbulls in their search for a nerve-steadying cup of tea!

Though we had berthed at 14.30 ship's time, the Finnish clocks were already showing 16.15. First and foremost, before the shops closed their doors, I had to find one or two small gifts for my family. Stockmanns is a complete department store that takes up most of a city block on Aleksanterinkatu. It is Finland's largest retail establishment. Here I found beautiful displays of crystal and artglass for which Finland is particularly famed. The stock of hand-made goods seemed to be the principal draw for the shop's foreign tourists — here colourful hand-woven textiles, ceramics, woodcarvings and reindeer hide boots, slippers and accessories came to the fore. After visiting the foreign exchange counter, I favoured purchases of Finnish metalwork jewellery.

As Swedish is an official language and spoken by eight per cent of Finland's 4.7 million population, I was not too surprised to find that numerous Helsinki street names were labelled in both Finnish and Swedish. Largely this 'second' tongue is spoken in the south and west regions of the country — the principal strongholds of the bygone Swedish occupation.

Mannerheimintie, or in Swedish Mannerheimvagen, is Helsinki's main thoroughfare. It is a broad tree-lined avenue that arrows directly through the central area and out to the main Turku road. The street is named in memory of Marshal Gustaf Mannerheim, Finland's military and political hero who fought to accomplish much during the infant years of independence. He was much loved by the Finns, becoming their President in the twilight years of his life. On his death in 1951 Marshal Mannerheim was given a full state funeral after lying in state in Helsinki Cathedral for three days. Fronting onto Mannerheimintie is a wide variety of places of special interest to Helsinki's many foreign tourists — the House of Parliament, National Museum, Finlandia Hall and Olympic Stadium.

In the late afternoon sunshine I trudged northwards along Mannerheimintie in prospect of including a glance at most of its attractions within a self-styled whirlwind city tour. The rush-hour traffic, both vehicular and pedestrian, was heavy and my progress was not as brisk as I had anticipated. During the weeks of mid-summer it is fashionable for Helsinkians to move out of town to nearby lake-side cabins or similar island residences. Usually, while the family enjoy the long summer days, the man of the house commutes daily to his city job. Each tea-time the scene is one of a mass evacuation to the country. Arriving at the imposing frontage of the granite-built Parliament House, I took stock of my time schedule and, allowing a space to visit South Harbour and Senate Square, abandoned the idea of venturing any further from the centre.

Across the broad highway an equestrian statue of Marshal Mannerheim stood proudly on a high plinth in front of the General Post Office. Though Helsinki is a city of vast architectural contrasts none of its buildings (taking the towers and spires of its ecclesiastical structures aside) rise to any great height. Thus one can walk the streets without feeling enclosed within a concrete sandwich. The Post Office was a substantial building by present-day styling but its low profile emphasised the advantage of the city's height regulations.

At the Central Station I stood back to digest the work of Eliel Saarinen. This massive creation was a product of the early 20th century when red granite was the fashion in Helsinki's building programme. In terms of sheer bulk it was most impressive; however, through a background of controversy and divided feelings, the building is often described as an unhappy one. My visit to the station was by way of an errand. In the giant main hall I found the Finnish equivalent to W. H. Smith where, at the counter, "English newspapers" was my request. I was offered two or three Sunday papers for which on my return to the ship the crew were most appreciative.

Finnish trains operate on a gauge of five feet — the very same as that of Russian railways. Although this extra-wide track did not catch my eye at the terminus, I did note the exceptionally low platforms at which the electric trains arrive.

Senate Square, hailed as one of the finest squares in Northern Europe, must be Helsinki's principal architectural showpiece. Designed by Engel exclusively in the 'Empire' neo-classic style, this perfectly balanced precinct looks as though it came straight out of a fairytale. The buildings aren't there just for their looks. Such important places as the Government Palace and the University occupy the east and west flanks respectively. At first glance one looks to be a mirrored reflection of the other. Columns and architraves in white, facings in gently spread pastel shades — I stood on the Cathedral steps and took in the quiet splendour of it all.

In marked contrast to the thronged commercial streets and boulevards, Senate Square was almost devoid of parked cars or moving traffic with its unrelenting auditory retort. Besides myself and a central bronze statue of Tsar Alexander II there was but a handful of people there to record the special beauty of these buildings in the light and shade of a semi-incandescent sun.

The Cathedral, dominating the square from a granite rock base thirty feet above it, rose skywards like a giant iced cake with green-coppered domes for added decoration. Within its snow-white walls the hush was more intense. Here I could not help reflecting back to my visit to the ship's engine-room that very same day — surely this was the extreme in audio contrasts! Compared to British Gothic masterpieces, the interior was distinctly plain, yet despite this smoothness nonethless eminent. Raised over the high altar was an elaborately framed painting depicting the suffering of Christ at Calvary. The organ formed a beautiful feature at the west end. It was sited on a sweeping gallery that overlooked the entire nave.

The Cathedral is sited in an area that has very much retained the flavour of the nineteenth century. As such this is the oldest standing part of the city. Through this comparative modernity Helsinki is often titled as the 'Daughter of the Baltic.' At the west end of the Market Square I was confronted with a circular fountain featuring a nude beauty named Havis Amanda. It was created by Vallgren in 1908. From then onwards the girl was adopted as Helsinki's 'Sweetheart;' she is said to symbolise the youthful city rising from the sea.

Here I was within sight and sound of South Harbour — the prominence around which present-day Helsinki was founded. Perhaps the water's edge is an unusual siting for a market place but forming the northern limit of the harbour there was no mistaking its importance to traders or buyers of both sea and land harvest. Facing onto the Market Square and across the sparkling water were many fine buildings — among them the Town Hall, the Supreme Court and further along the ceremonially guarded President's Palace — again inducing a scene from the last century. Between the boats and buildings, the cobbles are lined with neat rows of traders' stalls. Each morning, except Sunday, I understand the scene is one of colour and relentless activity amid eye-catching displays of fruit, flowers, vegetables and sea food. At evening time the thronged atmosphere is long passed — strolling the bare and empty cobbles with a small colony of white gulls I relied on imagination to capture the feeling of it all.

The harbour itself was busied with all manner of craft. Apart from being the embarkation place for Suomenlinna and other outlying islands, it is here that large ferry ships depart for Sweden and Germany — including the afore-mentioned 'Finnjet.'

I took the west side of the harbour favouring a steady walk along Helsinki's scenic waterfront as a means of journey back to the ship. Bowing from South Harbour to the main foreshore, the esplanade (Ehrenstromintie) carried me in view of the many off-shore trees and rock islands and islets. The prospect was more of a quiet and unspoilt lakeside than that of a far-reaching sea. There again, being virtually landlocked, low in salt content and having no tides to mention, I suppose the Baltic Sea has all the makings of an oversize lake anyhow. There are more than 30,000 islands around Finland's seaboard that, in forming a natural barrier against angry seas, provide an idyllic playground for boat owners and nature lovers alike. Allowing for the fact that the bulk of the country's population lives around the shoreline, it comes as no surprise to learn that the Finns take to the water as the British take to the roads. That Monday evening was no exception — beyond the promontory around which I strolled the shimmering sea was littered with small craft — yachts at anchor, motorboats weaving around the islands and dinghies coaxing the fickle breeze.

Facing the sea at that stage was a blend of fine buildings (this was a district where various foreign embassies are to be found) and the broad-leafed woodland of Kaivopuisto Park. This greener part of the city attracts Helsinki's many 'joggers' — a number of these 'keep fit' enthusiasts both young and old, male and female, I met en route.

Soon there were more boat landing places, small marinas and an intriguing type of jetty. Upon these square pontoons were three or four benches where both men and women scrubbed away at rugs, carpets and the like. These floor covering 'laundrettes' are a facility provided each summertime at all Finnish waterside towns. The idea stems back many generations and today, with a higher percentage of townspeople living within the confines of flats, is one that is still put to full use.

Having walked for some time and still out of striking distance I chose to take a taxi back to the ship. Here the non-English speaking manager of a waterfront filling station was of great assistance. On my stressing "Taxi — Baltic Enterprise" he jovially acknowledged with arm movements emulating the ship at sea then picked up the telephone. A large black Volvo pulled up on the forecourt within the minute.

'Enterprise' was so surrounded in activity that I had to pick my way through workers and vehicles both ashore and aboard. Sheepishly I crept into the dining saloon in hope of a belated dinner. It was near seven ship's time and I was aware that the usual assembly would have broken up.

Good fortune smiled upon me for I was not alone — Gerry Brazendale and Peter Green were sat together at the centre table. Having been greeted with the usual pleasantries I sensed that something was afoot.

"Had a good run ashore — how was Helsinki?" Brazendale asked. I gave a much abridged version of my flying visit commenting that I would have preferred to have seen the capital at a more leisurely pace.

"Well, it looks as though you will be seeing a little more of Finland than you expected." Peter Green's contribution came as the steward placed a dish of salmon salad before him.

At my arrival the Captain and Chief Officer had been going through a revised schedule of which orders had been received shortly after docking that afternoon. Due to a re-allocation of cargoes, our running sister 'Sirius' had been re-routed off her West Coast service and was heading for Helsinki in our wake. Following our call at Kotka the next day we were to make for the West Coast of Finland to take aboard 'Sirius's' England-bound cargo. In broad terms this meant additional calls at Turku and Mantyluoto involving four hundred miles of coastal sailing, a ship loaded to its limit and thirty-six hours delay to our return to England.

As mentioned at the outset the Finanglia services were at that time operating with one ship out of service. During the height of the summer holiday period, Finnish exports are at their lowest. Consequently, with small cargo commitments, this proves to be the most convenient time to carry out annual dry-dock surveys. At that very moment we were taking aboard London-bound cargo for the absent 'Baltic Progress' in addition to our normal shipment.

This deviation from Hull was already adding one extra day to the usual eight-day round voyage. Now this had been stretched further; it was a bitter pill to swallow for some of the crewmen who originally had hoped to start leave the coming weekend. Peter Green had been the one to pass on the glad tidings to his fellow mariners. He was now revealing their reactions to his Captain.

Brazendale become somewhat philosophical over the matter. "The dickens of this regular ferrying is that you begin to organise your life around its schedules. Really we should not depend on the ship adhering to its strict timetable but at some time or other we are all guilty of this. When something untoward happens involving even the shortest delay it can upset your whole domestic arrangements. Had we been deep-sea this temporary diversion would have gone more or less unnoticed. Sometimes on such a voyage an infringement of this nature can be rectified by speeding up turn-rounds later on. Short haul ro-ro's are run at optimum operational output. Whether at sea or in port there is no way in which two lost days can be made up. The only way to bring her back on time is to readjust the schedule."

From a passenger's point view such a change of plan is not an arguable issue. Conditions of booking clearly explain that in these circumstances there can be no grievances. In this instance both the Turnbulls and myself were more than happy to accept a more comprehensive cruise around Finland than originally planned. Indeed Bob and Ruth had decided to leave the ship at Purfleet instead of Hull returning home more or less on schedule. It would seem that I was the last to be informed. With a much appreciated meal inside me I joined a rather dismayed queue of crewmen at a quayside phone box awaiting to advise their families of our delayed return.

Whatever class or type of ship, responsibility for the day-to-day administration of the deck department rests on the head of the Chief Officer. Assisted by the Second and Third Officers he is answerable to the Master for the operational efficiency of all deck gear, the discipline, training and deployment of crew and, all important, ensuring that the cargo is loaded, stowed and discharged safely.

It was in the latter of these executive duties that Peter Green was engaged for most of that evening. On the news of our extended voyage he and the cargo superintendent had to rearrange the original loading plan. It was a matter of segregating the London-bound from the Hull-bound cargo at each port of call yet allowing the London consignment access to be discharged first. This was to pose a sticky problem when, later on, our holds and decks were to be crammed to capacity.

Sited at the after-end of the 'tween decks and overlooking the stern door aperture was a small control room. While working cargo, one of the three deck officers was to be found there. Seated at the control cabin's plate glass window, Green watched an intermittent flow of tractor-drawn containers roll aboard. At his right hand an array of coloured lights filled a bulkhead-mounted circuit board. As the ship lay at the quayside it was important to keep her on a level plane.

Green explained: "Should the ship be listing while being loaded, the stern doors, angled to the ramp, would be under tremendous strain resulting in serious damage."

Checking the ship's attitude as a heavily burdened trailer passed beneath the window, he reached to the illuminated control panel and activated the transfer of ballast from one area to another. The lights on the panel indicated the route along a network of arteries on which the water was being carried. "This fingertip control of trimming ship allows a substantial margin of flexibility when distributing the load. Theoretically we could almost fill the starboard cargo lanes and still ballast the ship level while the port side was empty."

At that stage an oncoming chain of containers was either being transferred by deck lift to the lower hold or raised through an opened hatch to be deposited on the weather deck by the ship's own gantry crane. At the lower level Willie Maclaughlan presided while the Finnish riggers cranked the lashing chains bar taught. Bernard Elworthy carried out similar duties in the fading Helsinki daylight above.

What were the containers carrying? Their gaunt steel sides displayed nothing bar a series of registration marks. Green was quick in blocking my inquisitiveness: "Scanning through the cargo manifest earlier on it looks as though there could be everything from machinery to mackintoshes! General cargo is the simple answer to your question. Tomorrow we shall be in the paper business. Kotka thrives round its saw mills and allied industries — we berth almost on the doorstep of a large pulp mill."

Apart from the bustling of the loading tractors, the quayside had been busied throughout by a fleet of articulated oil tankers. Each in turn, dwarfed by our soaring hull, levelled alongside and discharged its load through hefty pipes that disappeared through the port side bunkering door.

Despite the sustained efforts of all concerned we did not cast our mooring lines from the quays of West Harbour until 00.30 hours ship's time.

"We shall be lucky to be away by midnight," Peter Green had said when during the evening it was obvious that the re-allocation of cargo space was slowing the loading process. Indeed at 23.50 hours we saw a low-slung slave trailer decked with two 40 foot containers rumble aboard. This, perhaps the most formidable unit to be hauled up the ramp that day, concluded our Helsinki commitment.

Amid a flood of illumination both from aboard and ashore 'Baltic Enterprise' eased sedately from the quay. Heading stern first into the darkness, Gerry Brazendale eased the bulky ro-ro quietly past sleeping ships, factories and wharfs. At the main waterway she began to waken to the occasion. Her bow was turned to face the moonlit channel and, under the guidance of a local pilot, we started to retrace our steps back to Harmarja Island.

Once away from the high-pyloned illumination at the dockside the beauty of the night sky became the captivating element. In the not too distant north the summer sun had barely set before rekindling to the new day. Yet, in stark contrast above, and beyond to the southern extremities of the Baltic Sea, a powerful moon radiated an ice-cold phosphorescence amid a dark and starry sky.

While slowly drawing further from the twinkling lights of Helsinki's majestic waterfront, the promise of seeing night and day meeting in one sky became an ongoing realism. Across the city skyline rose an arc of light simulated within a vignette of prismatic colours. From a burnt-orange haze (against which the asymmetrical shapes of the stately buildings were silhouetted) the halo climbed through a delicate turquoise to a brilliant royal blue; directly overhead a more darkened blue was burnished by the moon's silver lustre. The aurora not only captured the undivided attention of the romantics aboard (a small group of spectators at the port rail included Bob and Ruth Turnbull, Clive Buchan, Peter Green and John Gunning), even the heads of the most hardened seamen were occasionally turned from their work on the mooring decks to marvel at its beauty.

Soon the ship turned her head to the south, leaving Suomenlinna on our port quarter. With several islands fronting the Helsinki backdrop the scene became more compulsive. The spread of water that now lay astern, ruffled only by our gathering wake, became a mirror to the overhead spectacle.

"I have seen this effect on many occasions but never more beautiful than this."

The statement came in broken English from our temporary navigator, who on completion of his assignment, was making for the lower decks.

While the ship hovered to accept the tiny pilot launch Harjarma lay close to starboard. Its squat lighthouse set amid the rocks steadily beamed forth alternate red and white warnings. To me the spotlight marked the culmination of a brief yet memorable visit to the Finnish capital — a visit indelibly etched within the framework of that idyllic departure.

With the pilot boat on its way to the island base, Brazendale pushed his engine controls meaningfully to the ten ahead reading. Above, responding in a business-like manner, the exhausts thrust sparks of ignited soot into the night air. In four short words the captain spelled out our immediate mandate — "We go to Kotka."

CHAPTER NINE

I woke to a silence to which I had not been accustomed aboard ship. On investigation I discovered that we were lying quietly at the Kotka ro-ro berth, brightly illuminated in morning sunlight. During the early hours, 'Enterprise' had devoured ninety or so sea miles arriving at Finland's largest export harbour complex before the working day had dawned.

Until such times as the cargo started to 'roll,' the ship was settled down to a rare interval of inactivity. Those who had stood watch through the night had grasped the opportunity of an unscheduled sleep — short as it would be. As for myself — I was soon dressed and treading lightly along the deserted alleyways en route for the lower decks.

Though I had been warned that our stay at Kotka was to be brief, I was determined to visit the town; even though this meant rising at an unsocial hour. In keeping with the general run of ro-ro berths, the Kotka terminal was a considerable distance from the main hub of the town. Lucklessly, as one would expect, transport to the town at that time of day was not in abundance. I am not averse to walking (having from time to time indulged in long distance walks of up to forty miles) so the prospect of a three-mile trek was no deterrent. Subsequently, putting my best leg forward I stole through the open stern doors on a pre-breakfast expedition.

At the berth directly ahead of 'Enterprise' with stern doors open for loading in the same manner was the green hulled 'Orion.' This was a twin sister of 'Enterprise' but from the Finnish side of the operation. On her run north she had initially hauled up from Felixstowe to Turku. After a coastal voyage of 270 miles she had arrived at Kotka several hours ahead of ourselves. 'Orion' was scheduled to depart for Felixstowe at mid-day.

Leaving the twin ships in readiness for their cargoes I moved away from the waterside scene. The harbour (Hietanen Satama) was one of Kotka's more recent port expansion projects. It was sited on what was once a close-shore island. A wide sweeping bight of new founded land carried a link road and railway towards the suburbs.

Working my way along this concrete strip I was confronted by a steady flow of traffic heading for the docks — the working day was about to start. With thoughts of the impending turn-round and the ship's departure I was induced to lengthen my stride. For such an early hour the sun was exceptionally hot. I began to boil and was compelled to cast down a lightweight rig — my wrist watch was barely reading 06.00!

Kotka, not usually projected as a key point upon the tourist map, is an unassuming coastal town of some 35,000 inhabitants that radiates an air of confident progress through a hard working background .It has developed around two islands at the mouth of the Kymi river. The islands are now permanently joined to the mainland by a series of road bridges and earthworks. The hub of the town is based on the most seaward area, this being Kotka Island.

My unfaltering stride hastened me along an irregular route that moved from the dock area through a residential suburb of variable housing and

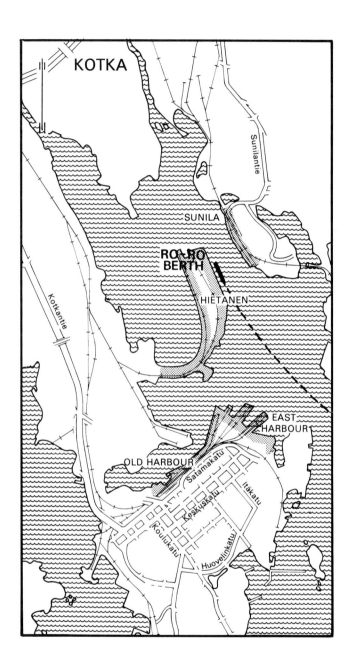

across the Kotka Island link into the town centre. Here I arrived among essentially modern streets favourably studded with broad-leafed trees that emitted the fragrance of the morning. I was pleasantly surprised to find an abundance of green areas. My meandering soon revealed tree-shaded boat harbours, playing fields with all the attendant facilities and parks and gardens where women had already started sweeping the footpaths.

Unlike Helsinki it was not a town of architectural gems. Largely due to the ravages of war Kotka had little to show me of its illustrious past. Though this historical background is shorter in time than that of other Finnish towns, it is perhaps of greater interest. Indeed, before the last decades of the 18th century the name of Kotka was only related to pasture, fishing waters and burn-beaten land.

However, after naval battles fought off its shores, the Russians observed that the area would be an excellent place to build fortifications against attacks from the west. Consequently they established a large garrison at the sea fortress of Svensksund. By 1802, showing the strategic importance the Russians attached to the area, the extended fortress had a population of some 8,000 people. When in 1809 Finland was ceded to Russia the fortress lost its military importance and Kotka was reduced to a shadow of its former self. Its population gradually declined and by 1836 this was estimated at no greater than 300. In 1855 during the Crimean War, a British naval force under the command of Captain H. R. Yelverton, bombarded the islands. The fortifications were totally destroyed and with the town burnt to the ground its few remaining people moved away.

Development of present-day Kotka commenced in the 1860's when the industrial revolution led to a massive upswing for Finland's woodworking industry. The utilisation of the Kymi river as a watercourse on which to float logs from the vast upland forests opened the way for the development of sawmills and the installation of a harbour at its Kotka estuary.

The sawmill and harbour town with its thousands of casual workers acquired at this time a reputation as a form of Finnish 'wild west.' It was a place where the working pace was high and wages were good — a place where the unsavoury recklessness of a 'Klondike' town was rife. Kotka was not transformed into an orderly community overnight — many decades were to pass before it established complete social reform.

Another chapter in Kotka's traumatic history was opened up during World War II when advancing Russian forces subjected the town to almost continuous bombardment. It is said to have been the most bombed point in Europe after Malta.

Post-war reconstruction was extensive; consequently the majority of buildings seen today came into existence within the past few decades.

Prior to departure the shelved volumes at my local reference library had little to offer by way of information about Kotka. It is a place that travel writers regularly describe as an industrial town and port having limited appeal as a tourist centre. Admittedly the town does revolve around its factories, sawmills and harbours — however any resemblance between Kotka and Northern England townships that came to fruition during the Industrial Revolution that I have frequented was only fragmentary.

One of the landmarks to which I trudged that Tuesday morning was the Old Water Tower. This was an octagonal cream-painted building crowned with a turreted look-out post not dissimilar in appearance to an ancient lighthouse. Set high above the trees on the rocky shelf of Haukkavuori it is recognised as one of the finest view-points in Southern Finland. It was from there that the whole plan of Kotka opened up; southwards and likewise to the west the Gulf of Finland was shimmering with its islands, skerries and infinite stretches of water that give Kotkans a natural playground for water-borne leisure activities. To the north and east occasional tall chimneys set around inroads of placid waters revealed the economic life-blood of the area. Close at hand and spread among the trees were the municipal and educational facilities of the town. Kotka boasts a variety of vocational training institutes including Finland's most modern navigational school and the country's only stevedore technical institute.

Back in town I walked in the parkland grounds of the Orthodox Church of St. Nicholas. Finland has two National Churches — the Evangelical-Lutheran Church of Finland, to which the main portion of the population belongs, and the Orthodox Church of Finland that accounts for a mere 1.5%, this being drawn mainly from the people of the eastern provinces.

Built in the classical style with a squat tower and dome, St. Nicholas's was one of two principal structures to remain after the days of the Crimean War, the other being the Imperial Fishing Cabin at nearby Langinkoski which was built by the Finnish government at the request of Tsar Alexander III. The Tsar much loved the area, spending regular summer holidays at the cabin in the late 19th century. Regrettably my schedule would not allow for a visit to the Cabin — owned by the Finnish government it has been preserved on its island site and opened to the public as a museum.

Soon Kotka seemed to come alive — the market place was a scene of bustling activity. Aside of heavily burdened vans and pick-up trucks, gaily awninged stalls were being erected and decked with all manner of garden produce. The streets were now filled with the sounds of traffic, people hurrying to work and shops opening for the day. Time was now passing quickly and I had to be getting back to the ship. Twice I stopped to ask the way but the use of the English language is not commonplace in Kotka. Nevertheless, on the tree-shaded patio of a modern coffee house I did manage to place an order for a glass of ice-cool milk and on consuming the same swayed the young waitress into telephoning for a taxi.

A ship's agent is someone who must be prepared to 'expect the unexpected.' It is his job to arrange for all the requirements a ship may need and any demands made on him by the master. This can cover a multitude of requests — at any hour seven days a week. Possibly a crew member may need medical attention or the master wants to recharge his float of ready cash or needs currency to cover a call on some foreign shore — stores, fresh water, fuel and repair facilities have all to be readily available. On top of this the agent has to be in constant contact with the ship, booking cargo, arranging storage and dealing with all the documentation concerning the cargo, including those demanded by the Customs and Excise.

Considering the number of off-beat jobs that can fall within his sphere of operation, arranging last-minute dental treatment for a face-sore member of 'Enterprise's' crew could not have been much out of the Kotka agent's morning routine.

Insignificant as it may be the discomfort of the cabin steward did delay our 10.30 ship's time scheduled departure to the tune of forty minutes. Cargo stowed and engines running, 'Enterprise,' poised to take on the 270-mile coastal run to Turku, had laid at the Hietanen harbour berth ready for sea for almost one hour before the steward (minus one tooth!) stepped aboard.

During this time, Brazendale had impatiently paced between bridge-house and starboard wing. From there, unwittingly patting the palms of his hands against the rail-top, he had more than a dozen times looked out over the close-by transit sheds towards the Kotka road. Anxious to get the great bulk of his charge thrusting westwards, he had called his deck crew to their stations shortly after the loading had been completed.

The additional voyage to Finland's West Coast was an occupational hazard that had to be contended with. For Brazendale this was the last of a three round-voyage session — he had been expecting to start leave on arrival at Hull late the coming weekend. Though he had not made it known at this stage, his annual family holiday had been arranged to commence around this timing. With something like thirty-six hours having been added to the voyage he had incurred problems far away from the job in hand. Equally, over the past two days he had had but a smattering of sleep and for him the prospect of any substantial rest period over the next two days was none the more encouraging. Now, as though this was not enough, he was being subjected to further frustration through a steward inconveniently deciding that he had toothache.

Moments after Brazendale had curtly asked Peter Green to "get on the phone and find out what the hell is happening," a dust-shrouded taxi swung round the sun-kissed sheds and drew to an abrupt halt on the concrete base way below. With the Master's eyes firmly glued to the accommodation ladder it was fortunate that the tall young man did not dally on the ascent.

With the pilot at his shoulder and voicing the usual litany of orders, Gerry Brazendale hurried 'Enterprise' from the ro-ro berth. Our mooring had flanked the west shore of a deep-water channel that flowed south for a couple of miles where it met up with the principal waterfront. Our sister ship 'Orion,' still in the throes of loading, was soon put on our starboard quarter — to port the giant Sunila cellulose works that had overpowered the west bank both by its appearance and unfortunate smell quickly fell beyond our now arrowing wake. Ahead, planed and polished as a sheet of glass, the Gulf of Finland again beckoned our ship's tireless energies.

Such was our departure from Kotka — a restless sun-baked occasion framed within a backdrop of Finnish industry.

In the heat of the day, visibility had deteriorated as not to allow a lingering onshore view of the town. Not that this disappointed the crew in any way. Apart from the unusually spectacular sky the previous night, hardly any of them warranted a second glance at anything that did not concern navigation. To them the everyday scene had no more significance than the wallpaper at home. For those who cared to look, the Old Water Tower provided our last visual contact with the shore. Its fresh cream painted dome gilded in diffused sunlight rapidly moved behind a curtain of sea haze that closed in all the more the further we travelled.

Had we been heading eastwards from Kotka we would soon have been sailing in Russian waters — the territorial boundary was a mere twenty-five miles away. On such a heading, Leningrad would have been looming up ahead by early evening. As things were, with the Kotka pilot on his way back to base, we were leaving longtitude 27 east on a heading of 230 with visibility under two miles. Despite the low level mist the sun baked our steel decks to the extent that regardless of footwear one sensed burning feet.

Along with several hundred tons of cargo our call at Kotka had produced two new passengers — Carl and Gillian. They were fortunate young Americans whom the pressures of time, finance and responsibilities had largely escaped. On a random visit to Europe they had worked their way north and east as far as political boundaries would allow. Having friends in London they were now poised for a few days break before heading for the Mediterranean. Rather than fly to London in less than three hours they were, in their words, "happy to take a novel way there" in more than three days!

Though Carl and Gill were 'travelling light' and were content to exist from day to day without alternating their mode of dress, a guitar was considered an essential part of the baggage. From Kotka onwards this guitar in the capable hands of Carl brought a new lease of life to the all-too-often fallible social atmosphere. Long sunny afternoons became flavoured with mellow tones of folk music drifting from here and there around the upper decks. In the evening the injection of live music prompted a sing-along party atmosphere in the smoke room. Most appropriately as I settled in a port-side deck chair that afternoon the tune was "We will sail away together"!

CHAPTER TEN

Turku is old and traditional and, having the distinction of being the former capital of Finland, holds a prominent place in Northern history. Unlike its successor, Turku was never founded; it developed naturally at the crossing of the Northern trade routes. The very word 'Turku' means a market or trading place.

Today Turku is an active commercial and industrial centre bounding with all the energies of modern living. Food, textile, precious metal and medical industries together with shipbuilding employ about half of the town's population of 160,000 — commerce almost one fifth.

Not the least of Turku's key-points of activity is its well tree-sheltered harbour. It is here that the ultra-modern ferries of the Viking, Silja and Bore Lines continuously manoeuvre to-and-fro on turn-round for either Stockholm or the Finnish-ruled Aland Islands.

Such is the number of ships involved on the many ferry routes between Finland and Sweden that one wonders how they can all cover their massive overheads. One indication is that, in comparison with everything else in Scandinavia, fares on these services are extremely cheap thus inducing a high volume of passenger traffic. A second piece of bait is said to be the low cost of duty free goods readily available for consumption aboard and to return home with. Even so it is more than surprising how two countries with a joint total population of only thirteen million can support up to thirty ferries trading between them.

The ferry scene on our arrival at Turku harbour was living up to its vibrant record. Two 'seal'-emblemed Silja and one red-hulled Viking Line ships busied about the quays that fronted the grey ramparts of the 13th century castle. It was early — 06.30 ship's time, 07.30 local; it was raining — sheeting down to be more precise. The obvious grey sky and accompanying poor visibility did nothing by way of promoting a favourable first impression of the port. The ferries offered the only splash of colour available at the waterside.

In retrospect the weather situation since leaving Kotka had been a recycle of that encountered while hauling northwards through the Baltic two days earlier — sparkling hot morning, sea-hazy afternoon leading to a foggy evening, overnight rain continuing through to a thoroughly miserable morning.

The 270-mile coastal voyage from Kotka had revealed little of Southern Finland. Had visibility been good we would have been treated to fine scenery as we passed and threaded by summer playground islands, boldly marked skerries and foremost promontories of the mainland.

Unfairly, both for passengers and navigators alike, this was not to be. Again as the weather thickened and the day wore on, Brazendale spent long hours pondering over radar and charts with his subordinates on the bridge. During the early hours of Wednesday morning he had brought 'Enterprise' to a near halt at the island of Uto — sixty-four miles south of Turku. It was here that we took on the Turku pilot — a short fair-haired man possibly in

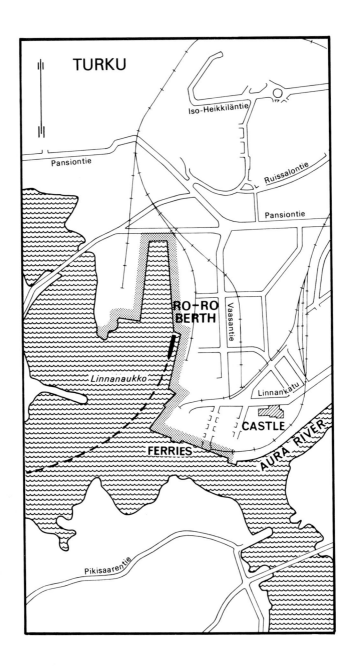

his late forties who immediately made his presence felt by shaking out his wet waterproofs in the centre of the bridgehouse carpet!

For five hours in half-light, fog and rain this man was to guide our ship through the hazard-strewn Turku Archepelago. Had it been any other person showering stone-cold rainwater about the bridgehouse at that early hour I feel sure there would have been some strong objections from the Master. As it was I sensed Brazendale was more than happy to welcome the pilot to his bridge despite his presumptuous entry.

The Turku Archepelago is claimed to be the most beautiful in the world. An outside chance of seeing dawn break over that island group had drawn me from my bed.

"I'm afraid you are going to be out of luck," Bernard Elworthy approached me in lament. "Judging from the report it is unlikely that the weather will pick up before mid-day."

Resigned to the fact that we were to thread through the Archepelago with very little visual contact, I returned to my cabin.

Sleep did not come easily. Two-minutely blasts from the fore-mast fog siren, course alterations which led to steady heeling first one way and then the other and occasional speed changes with subsequent variations in vibration frequency were no mean allies of an insomniac passenger. Thus 06.00 saw me once again planted in the bridgehouse port corner — by now to watch Turku arise out of the gloom.

At that time we were ghosting between two tree-clothed islands that narrowed the deep-water channel down to a slender river. Aside the tall pines (whose pyramid tops were hung in low mist) small sauna cabins rested at the water's edge. Each had a rickety plank jetty from which near-roasted bathers plunged naked directly into the cold depths. I was not surprised there were no such sights to be seen. Even the hardy Finns withdraw from taking 'pleasures' at such an early hour in unseasonal weather!

Soon the channel opened up into a huge, partially tree-fringed basin. At the far side were the ferries, cranes and sheds — Turku stood beyond them. There appeared to be an abundance of space for our ro-ro to manoeuvre and once more Brazendale, tired as he must have been, brought us to rest at a ramped berth on the main waterfront.

The call at Turku had been scheduled principally to collect empty containers and transport them to Purfleet as deck cargo The number of containers and trailers of the Finanglia circuit amounts to many thousands. Often some ports run up a surplus of empties and have to feed other bases that are running 'dry.' Regardless, the loading of the same would not take long and our stay at Turku was to be even shorter than that at Kotka. Any chance of a 'run ashore' looked more unlikely — so I began to think.

Over breakfast I decided that while the ship was slowly following the western coastline to Mantyluoto on the next leg of her voyage, I would make the journey overland. This would allow me a little time to spend in Turku and the opportunity to see something of the Finnish countryside. Erik Nasman from the ship's agents enthusiastically gave me details of

117

coach services to the north and I accepted his offer of a lift into town.

By 11.00 local time, thirty or so containers had been stacked aboard and the deck crew were at their stations. The customary departure signal bellowed out and, from the shelter of his quayside parked car, Erik and I watched as the now load-banked 'Enterprise' crept from her Turku berth. Her screws bit the water with vengeance thrusting that now familiar grey hull into a clockwise motion. Showing us her twin stern doors she ploughed away across the harbour hurriedly disappearing from view behind a screen of tall pines. It was estimated that she would take between six and seven hours over the 111 sea miles to Mantyluoto ('Manty' to those on board); the coach journey that I was to take would amount to three hours. I expected to be reunited with the ship and my companions in time for dinner.

Turku (Abo in Swedish) is straddled either side of the Aura River, the mouth of which forms a sizeable part of the harbour complex. Our route to town followed in close company with the Aura and this provided the chance of a close look at the thronging ferry terminals plus, a little further upstream, a string of crane-swarthed shipyards.

From the tourist's point of view the principal attraction there was sited on a lawned banking taking command of both river and harbour — namely Turku Castle. Having been subjected to a long history of fires, siege, misuse and dereliction, the castle was eventually restored to its heyday glory through a scheme that commenced shortly after the Second World War and took more than twenty years to complete.

The building dates back to the thirteenth century when it was built as a fortress to guard the trading town of Turku. As Finland was by then part of the Kingdom of Sweden, the castle became favoured by visits from the monarchs of that land and subsequently its accommodation was enlarged. At one period in the sixteenth century, it was occupied by Erik XIV who at the time was pressing for the hand of Queen Elizabeth I. This man was soon to be dethroned by his brother Duke John and actually imprisoned at Turku. Together with a comprehensive historical museum, the restored castle offers its visitors a glance of the opulent Renaissance style rooms in which the royalty of that era dwelt. But the castle is not just a monument to the years gone by, for it is widely used by the people of Turku for all manner of cultural and social occasions — banquets and concerts are often held there, even wedding receptions are catered for.

Close by the first bridge up river was moored the Finnish Naval Training Frigate 'Suomen Joutsen.' She was at the opposite bank to which we were travelling. Erik slowed so that we could obtain a clear view of her from the broad riverside concourse. Against a backcloth of green foliage this beautiful square-rigger showed her white hull, tall masts and far-reaching yard arms in splendid profile. I only wished we had been seeing her under full sail out in the Baltic (a full rigger at sea is one nautical joy which to date has eluded my eyes).

From the riverside a brief drive along tree-shaded streets took us to the wet cobble-stoned market square. On receiving final directions from Erik, I expressed my thanks, bade farewell and watched as his small saloon disappeared among the mid-morning traffic.

Onwards, from a visit to an ultra-modern bank to replenish my pocket with Finnish marks (this for some unknown reason took far longer than I had anticipated); much of my short stay at Turku was spent meandering around the city centre — lucklessly trying to avoid the raindrops! Department stores, gift shops and both outdoor and covered markets were heavily thronged with shoppers. Despite the weather, the place bubbled with atmosphere. Apart from the Orthodox Church at the top of the square, the buildings in that area were mostly modern. Regardless, in standing with the great distinction of being a former capital city, Turku generated an air of maturity. In likeness to Helsinki, the streets ran very much in sequence. Indeed the street plan of central Turku looks something like a section of graph paper — many parallel lines running at right-angles to each other. Had there been two or three days at my disposal the streets would have led me around a city more than amply furnished with tourist attractions.

Turku is one of the principal Swedish-speaking strongholds on the Finnish mainland. I say mainland, for the entire population of the Finnish Aland Islands that lie half-way to Sweden speak nothing but Swedish. It is said that in the bi-lingual towns which are mostly situated on the southern and western coastlines, there is a low birth and high emigration rate among the Swedish-speaking Finns. From my experience I feel Turku is best described as tri-lingual for nowhere (in marked contrast to Kotka) did I find difficulty in communicating with the 'locals.'

Gone lunchtime the clouds began to give way to a lazy sun. The predictions had been accurate but this was no consolation. It was time for me to be moving on.

The conductress on the coach was particularly helpful. It seemed that on the inter-town services these smartly uniformed girls care for their passengers in the manner of an air-hostess; helping the aged to their seats, attending to the baggage that was stored in an area free of seats at the rear of the vehicle and announcing our arrival at various points en route. At 14.30 the engine struck up and from my window seat I watched as we whisked by the main railway station and its attendant marshalling yards. Ten minutes later we were drawing away from Turku's suburbs on a well-surfaced highway that undulated towards pine-covered countryside. The coach was headed for Pori, a town of some 70,000 inhabitants situated twelve miles from the coast. At Pori I was to change onto a local bus service that would take me westwards to Mantyluoto.

At 130,085 square miles, Finland is one of the largest countries in Europe. It also lies entirely north of latitude 60 degrees N., which inevitably means long hard winters. These two factors pose a special problem with regard to transport, for the country's economic stability relies greatly upon a satisfactory year-round transport system.

The earliest snowfall comes to the far north in September or October, and by Christmas the whole land is under snow. In the south the white carpet can stay anywhere between three and six months at a depth of one to three feet, above the Arctic Circle it lasts between six and eight months. When the snow arrives twenty-five per cent of private motorists garage their cars until spring; the remainder fit special winter tyres and for several cold months become proficient at four-wheel ice skating!

By November the average temperature for the day drops below zero centigrade and remains so until April. February is the coldest month when the day's average is around —10 centigrade. Records show that the minimum temperature for that month varies between —24 and —40 degrees centigrade. During the winter freeze-up, which penetrates the ground to a depth of between one and three feet, Finland's 2,500 miles of inland waterways are toally unusable. Throughout this time the country's powerful icebreakers strive around the coast to keep open the south-west ports in all but the hardest weather (Mantyluoto is considered the northernmost winter port). But the Finns' most formidable task is that of clearing their 44,000 miles of public roads. Snow ploughs are followed by road planes with serrated blades that keep the ice or snow layer at a suitable thickness. Though this must make car riding somewhat bumpy, the grooves made by the plane prevent side to side skidding.

It is estimated that six million cubic feet of snow and ice are removed from Finland's roads each winter and that over one million tons of sand and salt are spread on them. In carrying out this work the vehicles involved travel up to six million miles. On the bonus side, frost penetration creates greater load-bearing capacity. Often heavy transport can be driven on roads that are classed as unsuitable, soft ground and even swamps. In some cases snowploughs work their way across the ice to inhabited islands in both sea and lakes. At a certain point on the Gulf of Bothnia between Finland and Sweden a road is cleared across the ice and substitutes for the ferry service that links the two countries.

The journey to Pori was on well-founded roads that ran straight for miles on end. On some stretches road gangs were busy patching and resurfacing— ominous of the departed winter's toll. Away from town traffic density was low. At times we could be travelling on open highway without sign of another vehicle. Here and there the coach would pull off the main route onto unsurfaced roads that led through small villages of gaily painted wooden houses. On making its call, which was sometimes to deliver (or pick up) packaged goods rather than passengers, the coach would wend its way back to the trunk road and speed away. At one stage, following one hour of travel, we halted for a break at a combined cafe, filling station and roadside stores fronted by a shale track that was heavily puddled. I tagged on with the twenty or so passengers who made pilgrimage across the waterborne car park to the cafe ('Baari' is the Finnish name for such an establishment) and contributed to the depth of red mud left in the doorway. Worthy of note is the Finnish practice of hanging exterior doors to open outwards. This I understand is to prevent snow falling inside when the door is opened. Personally I see problems here with deep snow or high winds!

Through the coach window the countryside seemed generally low lying

— in some places decidedly swampy. Often there were smallholdings that looked to profit on a small herd of cattle and a few acres of root crops. The south-west is known to be one of Finland's principal agricultural areas but nowhere did I see any evidence of large-scale farming. Ironically Finland has far more arable land than it needs. Over recent years when, through the the introduction of modern techniques, output has increased more than consumption, large areas of farm land have been made redundant. Here the problem facing agricultural experts has been to identify the least efficient cultivated land and allocate it for other use.

There were coniferous trees; there had to be, it would not have been Finland without them. Yet it was not the virile forestry as found in the vast upland regions that provide for fifty-five per cent of the country's total exports. The glades of pine, spruce and fir which spread their way down to the roadside were purely characteristic of the area — pleasant woodland of more visual and recreational value than of use to a vigorous industry.

Similar in meaning were the occasional stretches of water which offered quiet relief to the green landscape. This was not part of Finland's Lake District; literally we were far from it. Eight per cent of the country's surface area is covered by water and this is concentrated within a vast interior region where lakes are counted in their thousands. Away from Finland there are few places in the world where land and water are mingled so freely. I am more than conscious of the fact that the small lakes and pinewoods seen that afternoon were only an entree to the true Finnish landscape: without them the journey would have been all the poorer.

On face value there was nothing ostentatious about Pori. Its unglamorous town centre buildings conformed to a certain uniformity generally accepted as the norm when away from the main tourist centres. For me places like Pori (and Kotka) exemplified the backbone of the Finnish ego. Honest, hardworking industrial communities with a determination to progress regardless of all adversity. It would be fair to say that Pori has had its share of adversity, for, since being founded in 1558 at the mouth of the Kokemaenjoki River, the town has been ravaged by war and burned many times. Having been devastated by fire in 1852 an extensive rebuilding plan was made and this contributes greatly to the town's character today. One of the features of that period from which Pori still benefits is a group of riverside houses; they are claimed to be one of the country's loveliest architectural sights.

The service bus to Mantyluoto roared, bumped and rattled its way out of town with barely a handful of passengers. Soon it was amid flat featureless country that provided little more than swampy grazing land for equally miserable looking cattle. This was not one of Finland's high-spots, least of all a grand finale to my visit. But when one realises that in years long past much of the area was under the sea one cannot cast aspersions on it. The shore-line of West Finland is going through a slow process of elevation and consequently the sea is withdrawing. Today Pori is much more detached from the sea than say in 1842 when it boasted the country's largest mercantile fleet.

121

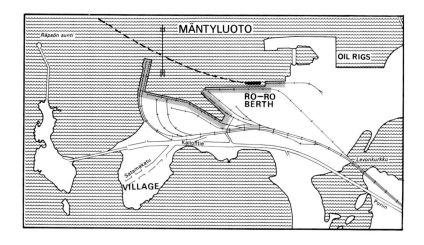

Few would choose to visit Mantyluoto unless they had business there. For the tourist there is little other than a straggling village of wooden houses, an old stone pier and a long intriguing name. Once a close-shore island, the area (known to the people of Pori as 'Sea Pori') is now linked as an irregular peninsula of land that lends itself to sea-borne industries. Though open westwards to the Gulf of Bothnia, tree-fringed islands group around the near waters to form what one could describe as a natural harbour. Mantyluoto is a place of wide open spaces. Acres of dockland are regimentally linked with railway trucks, timber stacks, oil drums and containers. Unlike most ports the transit sheds do not crowd the waterfront. Not as though there are many sheds but what there are lie widely spaced some distance from the ships. The commanding visual factor at Mantyluoto harbour however is not the commercial dock. Large-scale construction of oil rigs and platforms is a booming industry there and effactually dominates the skyline.

The bus driver motioned that we had reached the terminus. It had to be me he was beckoning for by now I was the only passenger remaining. I stepped down onto a roadway of compressed shale and waited as he swung the utility vehicle around a marked turning circle and started back for Pori. He had little alternative; the only option open from there was the sea. As the bus faded into the distance I began to take stock of my new surroundings.

Ahead a line of dockside cranes scribed out the waterfront and that obviously was where I needed to be. Peering between massed regiments of railway trucks and containers as I walked, I could see the superstructure of two or three ships but certainly nothing answering to the description of 'Baltic Enterprise.' Fair enough, the time had only reached 16.45 local, so my ship was hardly due yet — six to seven hours from leaving Turku at 11.00 I had been told. All the same in such an outpost as this I would have felt all the happier had she been already moored at the quay with what I eventually made out to be two Russian freighters and a small gravel dredger. It was so noticeably quiet; the swishing of grass and rustle of stray pieces of litter blown by a warm onshore breeze were the only sounds. There were no people either; up to that point I had not met anyone or in fact seen anyone. It was as though this far-flung place had been evacuated.

Cautiously I approached the only building of substance in the immediate area and found that it was the offices of a Finnish shipping company. Inside the hollow foyer I waited at an empty desk for what seemed like an hour. When at long last a middle-aged lady made an appearance behind the desk, I was foiled by a language barrier. Communications were bad — non existent to be more accurate. Eventually two of the good lady's colleagues arrived from back stage and joined in a good-humoured bout of arm gesticulating and ship sketching.

From this session of Anglo-Finnish charades I established that they knew of the ship 'Baltic Enterprise' though they had not seen here at Mantyluoto for many months. They were not aware that she was due to arrive that day but if she were to do so she would use a berth at the far end of the dock close by the oil rig construction area. Surely 'Sirius' was the ship currently operating on the U.K. service?

Obviously this was not the Finanglia agent's place of business but the people there had been helpful and I now knew in what direction to head. On declining their offer of a seat until such times as they closed for the day, I made off for the corner of the dock where steelwork towers and gantries overshadowed all else.

From what I could see there were two oil rigs under construction at the harbour. One was a five-legged job, nearing completion and already in the water. The other, still in its infancy, was cradled by the gigantic cranes, jigs and other miscellany that adorned the yard. This was a thrusting industrial complex which, with its noisy machinery, clattering of metal surfaces and sparking welding torches, contrasted greatly with the still slumbering dockyard. I stared in amazement at the size of the rigs. When on station they present an awe-inspiring sight but when in harbour their fully revealed enormity is no less than staggering.

Three-quarters of a mile on from the office block, I arrived at what was unmistakably a ro-ro ramp. There were many U.B.C. containers around too and I decided that I had found the berth. Unfortunately it was an empty berth as was the bay and the open waters beyond. Sat on a mooring bollard I gazed out to sea and reviewed the situation.

Had I made a grave mistake by leaving the ship — time was rolling on and still there was no sign of her or any indication that she was about to arrive. Equally none of the few people I had so far met had any knowledge that 'Enterprise' was expected.

Could there have been yet another change of orders and she was now heading for London without me? — or could there have been a mechanical failure and she had limped back to Turku? At 61 degrees N. I was further north than at any other time in my life and, apart from a few unused Finnmarks and my passport, I only had with me what I stood up in. Surely in the event of me being stranded so the agent would have been informed and would send someone to find me. If not? — Peter Green had made mention of a hotel somewhere around here; perhaps I could have a meal there and make a telephone call?

While lonely mulling over these probabilities in what had turned out to be a clear summer evening, I became conscious of the dockside awakening from its siesta. Tractor engines were being started, cars were arriving and people were making for the quay. Soon this build-up of activity had reached epidemic proportions and it became all too obvious that a ship was expected.

Within minutes the growing apprehension of the last hour or so had been dismissed. From behind the screen of 'Manty's' stone pier, the ship that silently entered the bay was clearly 'Baltic Enterprise.' And what a memorable picture she made too, silhouetted before a diminishing sun while framed between outlying islands.

It was now plain to see that I had arrived at the dock during a work break period that continued until such times as the ship was about to berth. The 'jungle telegraph' had given the alert and now the people who were arriving from nowhere (some were women with clipboards in their hands) were here to work an evening shift.

A remote harbour on the West Coast of Finland is not a place one would expect to be savouring the most traditional of all English dishes. Having been prepared and cooked by experienced hands, the roast beef and Yorkshire pudding proved to be firm favourite on the dinner menu.

Showered and changed, I had joined the assembly which at the sound of the dinner gong filtered into the immaculately laid saloon. On the Master's instructions, the meal had been delayed thirty minutes. He did not make a regular habit of this but in this instance the docking operation had clashed directly with the usual meal time; this slight change in the domestic schedule was definitely not for the benefit of a stray passenger who had been roaming the countryside for almost two hours — nonetheless I did find it highly convenient!

Whether it was because we were soon to be homeward bound or simply that we were resting at a quayside I do not know but this was one of the more appreciated meal times. Much for my benefit and those having the off-watch siesta, the conversation at the centre table revolved around the voyage from Turku. To the accompaniment of structural shuddering induced by the below decks loading, I listened to the reasons for the ship's late arrival.

A course had been set by the Turku pilot that carried the ship to the pilot base at Isokari Island. A fault had developed on the pilot launch and it was some time before the pilot could leave the ship. Throughout this time, Brazendale had held 'Enterprise' stationary entirely by engine manipulations. "We wasted a lot of time there. I was on the verge of bringing the pilot with us to 'Manty' when a second boat put out to collect him." Brazendale jovially emphasised that it was within his power to do such a thing.

From then on, by laying off courses of 314, 015 and 051, he had worked 'Enterprise' up the coast in a most time-saving manner. This route had brought her past some of Finland's finest holiday beaches, but most significant of all she had hauled close by the port of Rauma. It was here, of course, that 'Enterprise' was built and completed in 1973.

"Bet you were beginning to sweat a bit when we didn't turn up on time. Great place to be stranded at, this 'Manty.' Think of theatres, restaurants and night clubs you have here!" John Garvey added to the conversation in his usual satirical tone.

Oddly enough it was not long after dinner that I left the ship for the second time that day. Nils Pettersson, an official at the dock, had heard of my interests and came aboard to invite me along to see his home and family. Departure time had provisionally been set for midnight, ship's time — I could just squeeze in a two-hour visit, so I gladly accepted. We had barely motored five miles when the tall young Finn swung the car off the main road and headed on an unsurfaced track towards a secluded residential estate. Nils's home was something rather special on account that he had constructed most of it himself. Set on an elevated site among tall pines, the timber-built house was of his own split-level design.

Indoors the decor and furnishings were very much of the modern Scandinavian style. The principal living area was concentrated on the upper level. Here open planning, solid timber panelling and concealed lighting were put to full effect.

Below was the leisure area which incorporated an indoor sauna cabin with shower and changing rooms, a cosy bar that was centred around an open fireplace and a children's play corner. There were utility rooms for laundering and storing bulky winter clothing. Racks contained skis for each member of the family.

Finns rely on a high level of insulation to keep their homes warm through the long hard winters. Often walls have several skins that sandwich layers of specially processed insulation material. Triple glazing is becoming commonplace and I understand government legislation is to demand this on all new buildings.

Nils's home had all the latest insulation within its walls, roof and floor as protection against the severest of frosts. Naturally there was an equally efficient central heating system that was fed on electricity. Incidentally electricity comes at a much lower cost to the Finns than it does in the U.K.; therefore it is widely used as a domestic heating fuel.

After I had been shown over the house, Nils's wife produced coffee, biscuits and Finnish cheese at a candlelit table. My patchy visit to their country was rapidly drawing to a close; for this final display of hospitality I was extremely grateful. Typical of their breed, the Petterssons were hard working people. They had extended a great deal of effort and sacrifice to set up their home — a house suitable for Ideal Homes Magazine.

125

CHAPTER ELEVEN

We carried from Finland that night an almost capacity load of general cargo. Both weather and after decks were built up with a miscellany of containers; below, six lanes of heavily burdened slave trailers pushed back from each 'tween deck to within feet of the securely rammed stern doors. 'Enterprise' was now drawing twenty-one feet of water. As an effect of this load, her maximum speed had been reduced by one knot.

On drawing out of Mantyluoto harbour, all five passengers stood at the after rail. Not that there was anyone at the quayside to wave goodbye to; we were out of bed purely to witness our departure from that country of the North. It was dark and, for the first time that week, decidedly chilly. Carl's guitar murmured out melancholy chords that registered with the mood of the occasion.

Having slipped our ropes, the shore-crew had vanished into the night, leaving the powerful overhead floodlights there to beam down on lifeless concrete. Nursed further and further from the berth, our ship gradually inched her bow towards open water. Soon the old stone pier was slipping beyond the port quarter. We continued at a snail's pace for a mile or more until the bobbing light of the pilot launch that had fussed about us headed back for the shore.

Carl's rendition of 'Yesterday Once More' was suddenly swamped by the chant of thunder that ripped out of the funnel-top. Simultaneously, despite the darkness, the black water beneath the stern was visually transformed into a foaming liquid mass. Slowly the floodlit arena diminished to an eerie glow on an invisible horizon. The courtesy flag was lowered. Finland was gone — we were homeward bound.

By early morning the chart showed that we had carved 120 miles south-westwards across the Gulf of Bothnia and come to within twelve miles of the Swedish coast. This was the first leg of a 700-mile run we faced down the Baltic that would take an estimated 40 hours. For much of the first half of that voyage we would be sailing 100 miles to the west of our outward course. Later in the day this new route would carry us southwards along the west coast of Gotland, the Baltic's largest island.

In the meantime, having turned port onto 144 degrees at the Grund-kallen Light, we spent the breakfast hour slipping between Sweden and the Finnish Aland Islands. Said to contain some 6,000 islands, the Aland group links with that of Turku. Mariehamn is situated at the south-west corner of the staggered 30-mile long main island. It is to here that the ferries from both neighbouring shores bring many thousands of holidaymakers each year. One of Mariehamn's main tourist attractions is a maritime museum that features the famous windjammer 'Pommern.'

This was to be a day of plain sailing, a day free of pressing commitments and unexpected diversions. Having been given a loose rein, the ship had settled to the task of eating up the Baltic's lonely miles. Though she was nearing her deadweight limit and making $17\frac{1}{2}$ knots, there was no outward indication of her being under stress. If anything there were signs to the contrary — with her propellers sunk deeper below the surface there was unquestionably less underfoot vibration and equally the accommodation block was enjoying a quietness over and above the norm. Discounting any untoward events there was every chance that she would put on more than 400 nautical miles behind her in the course of the next 24 hours. She had done this many hundreds of times before and was more than capable of repeating the performance.

Conditions were good. At long last we had shaken off the dreaded sea mist that had inhabited the northern Baltic for the past three days. Today it was a deep blue Baltic, a sea that stretched to a hard unbroken line that ringed the 360 degrees around us. It was a sea bearing no spite or vengeance; to the set pattern of its oncoming corrugations we rolled gently at an agreeable frequency.

Mid morning arrived and we levelled with the Market Lighthouse. At this stage we had completed the last limb of a 100-mile 'dog leg' around the Aland group. Willie Maclaughlan, alone and master of all before him, re-adjusted the auto-pilot. In response the ship's head smoothly crept round to starboard until it settled on 208 degrees. There it was locked and there it would stay for the next 300 miles.

We were at sea and both ship and crew seemed content to be there. There was good reason to be so. In a period amounting to little more than 48 hours we had berthed at no less than four ports. For much of this time visibility had been poor — coastal navigation is a strain. 8,000 tons of varied cargo had pounded back and forth, up and down. Dozens of people — workers, officials and visitors — had tramped around the decks and along the alleyways. Almost every single mechanical system had been fully employed. Paperwork had been in abundance. In the course of these events eight different pilots had been aboard, eight attendant launches had drawn alongside.

This was a day when both ship and crew could go about their work unhindered by the pressures of port. And doing this they were.

At times like this, three or four able-seamen would spend much of the working day with paint brushes in their hands. Bulwarks, rails, super-structure and decks — every square inch of the mass of external steelwork needed a periodic coat of paint. 'Enterprise' was no longer a new ship; the elements were her enemies. As each winter retreated, the effects of her exposure to wind and rain, ice, frost, salt and grime were more than evident. Each year the task of obliterating the rust streaks became greater. It was the Chief Officer's responsibility to arrange a schedule that systematically brought the ship back to her former glory. If weather conditions had been favourable the painting would be well advanced by mid summer. In following this programme, the Bo'sun would each day gather his men at the paint store and issue out gallons of white, green or maybe grey. From there they would make off to whichever was the lee-side of the ship and set to work with roller and brush. The external surface of the hull was, of course, a separate entity and, when at sea, unavailable for painting. This was a job that had to be carried out whilst the ship was dry-docked. Then one would

127

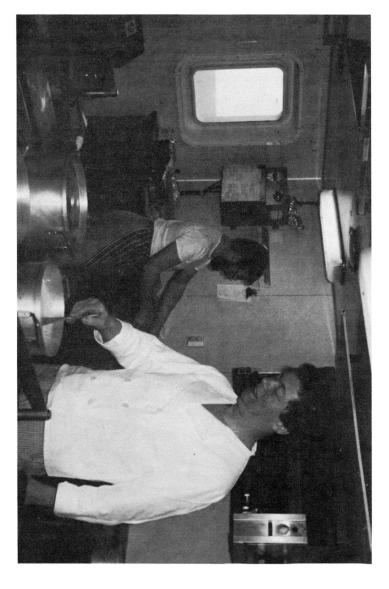

Richard Oakley (left) and John Jubb at work in the galley.

see the seamen at the quayside busily occupied with long-handled brushes or rollers coating grey paint over the rubs and grazes that inevitably accumulate through repetitive berthing and scrubbing against lock walls.

That Thursday morning a fresh green carpet of paint was being laid on the main deck's port side. Simultaneously, in a more artistic vein, Bo'sun Edwards worked off a scaffolding that had been erected alongside the funnel housing. There, in red, buff and white, he freshened up the large U.B.C. 'anchor and chain' motif that embellished the upper superstructure.

It was the main deck 'wet paint' barrier that halted my morning ramble at the opened galley door. Through that portal zealously employed in an overbearing temperature were Head Cook John Jubb and Second Cook Richard Oakley. Chef's 'special' on the lunch menu was to be grilled pork chop, apple sauce, potatoes, sprouts etc. Along with the entree, cold table and dessert, the main course preparation was in its final throes. Though the hands of the wall clock crept close to lunch hour the two white-garbed cooks moved between the large centre island stove, worktops and store cupboards with unrushed control.

John Jubb had been head cook aboard 'Baltic Enterprise' since her maiden voyage. He was a lean six-footer with a fresh complexion and jovial disposition. His bright personality matched the quality of his cuisine — without question he was well-liked throughout the ship.

"It pays not to cross the cook!" was his flippant reply when earlier I had challenged him with this statement. In all frankness, John Jubb openly believed that a well-fed crew is a happy crew. In adhering to this principle, he had earned great esteem among the fraternity with whom he sailed.

Richard Oakley was a fellow who backed Jubb in a certain unpretentious manner. Doctrined by the noise, heat, pressure and often angular difficulties of work in a floating kitchen, Oakley voiced his opinions accordingly. Being Jubb's understudy, Oakley was allowed the distinction of becoming head cook whenever leave commitments determined this. During the period either of the two men were ashore a third member of the team (assistant cook) filled the gap. On this voyage it was his turn to be absent.

Lacking nothing by way of latest domestic gadgetry, the face of the galley was that of any modern catering unit. Its spaciousness led one to believe that it had a capacity to cater for a number of people far in excess of the thirty-one aboard. Naturally there was a strong accent on cleanliness and hygiene; here I felt the 'Enterprise' galley superseded standards often not met in shore establishments.

After being wakened by the watchkeeping seaman at 05.30, the cook's working day was soon to start. At 06.00, priority was given to baking the day's bread-rolls. One hour later early breakfasts would be the order and this meal continued in patchy fashion until the saloon tables were cleared at nine. Having already worked out the lunch menu with the catering officer, there was no hesitation in starting with the vegetables, timing the roast and making headway with soups, salads and desserts. There was a two-hour break at 13.00 after which dinner became of over-riding importance.

My visits to the galley were never prolonged. It was an area where the intensive efforts of those employed within left a slothful passenger feeling somewhat guilty. Equally, being an environment of hotplates and ovens, mincers and mixers, knives and butchers' blocks that could roll or pitch at the whim of the ocean, it held latent perils for the unaccustomed.

Unless one moved fluidly around the ship, it would have appeared unlikely that she could be carrying a crew of twenty-six. But twenty-six there definitely were. These men had a rigid pattern of commitments that spread them diversely between galley and radio room, bridge and engine room. The often empty decks, lounges and alleyways laid emphasis on these work arrangements. Also contributing to the scarcity of stairway traffic was the upstairs-downstairs situation that segregated officers and seamen. Totalling fifteen men, those who inhabited the lower accommodation were socially apart from the rest of the ship. Away from their work, stewards, cooks or seamen were never seen above main deck level. Theirs was a separate world to which after the arena of watch-keeping, dish washing or stewarding, they retreated.

The seamen's accommodation area was a region that had always escaped the infiltration of passengers and was likely to remain so. In this respect, as a passenger occupying some of the grandest quarters aboard, dining with the senior officers and making note of all before me, it was naturally not easy to become accepted when invading this stronghold. Individually I had arrived on equal terms with the more senior men there. But looked upon as an alien from above, collectively my presence was regarded with astute suspicion. This in no way relegated my admiration of the role the seamen play. I am more than conscious of the fact that without their labours the ship could never put to sea. Often diminutive in the privileged eyes of those in higher orders, such work as greasing, dish-washing or painting is no less a seagoing necessity than the more glamorous occupational involvements in the engine control room or bridgehouse.

There was no wastage of labour. To keep the ship on an incessant course of cargo ferrying the presence of each and every man was essential; in context it was a team in which all from Master to pantry boy played a vital role. Though the traditional divisions of rank were in full effect, there was no apparent undertow of disapproval. All knew it was the occupational responsibility attached to a crewman's work that determined his station aboard.

During the course of that Thursday afternoon I was to see for the first time an assembly of the full crew. In this I witnessed an occasion where officers and men were side by side physically involved in a common cause.

Whilst at sea there were the odd occasions when one was startled from study or sleep by the fixed clamour of an emergency alarm system. So finely balanced was this warning arrangement that even the slightest misbehaviour of an electronic or mechanical unit took on the publicity of a major breakdown.

More often than not this was identified as something of little significance and within minutes silence reigned along the alleyways once more.

Lifeboat drill, starboard-side boat deck.

On a sunny afternoon, in mid Baltic, with no sight of other shipping, no sign of land, 'Enterprise' was cleaving an arrow-straight road of bubbling wake that lingered astern seemingly as far as the deep blue horizon. Closed cabin doors indicated that a number of those aboard were taking the opportunity of a brief siesta. An idyllic sea-going situation to which one could not foresee any immediate change; indeed all appeared to be well. Yet the peace that surrounded that afternoon was soon to be irrepairably broken by the fearsome belling of the alarm. This was not the usual evocative warning for the continuous racket had been preceded by seven short blasts.

I was one of several people who, reacting to the alarm, emerged from their quarters donning a bulky bright-orange lifejacket. At the after rail I was ushered to the boat deck where on the starbord side a mixed group of crewmen were rapidly uncovering a white and orange hulled lifeboat. Having been reduced to slow ahead, 'Enterprise' wallowed aimlessly at the will of a lethargic Baltic tempo. A gathering of some twenty lifejacketed people stood back while Peter Green took charge of the situation. On his commands a carefully drilled team lowered the davit beams from which the boat was suspended. Two decks above pacing the bridge wing, Gerry Brazendale was observed to look at his wrist watch. He was there alone. All three of his deck officers were by now involved in the boat launching.

As the lifeboat levelled with the green deck and overhung deep water, Bernard Elworthy and an able-seaman urgently scrambled aboard. There was room enough for 38 people aboard that craft but today its capacity was restricted to two men. Several moments passed as adjustments were made to both davits and release lines, then all heads craned over the rails as three tons of lifeboat jerkily made a twenty-foot drop towards the ocean.

I was not witnessing the casting adrift of two insubordinate crewmen! It was simply a weekly exercise at which regulations demanded the attendance of everyone aboard. Together with several inflatable life-dinghies and rafts, we were carrying two such conventional motorised lifeboats. At the most appropriate period of the week, the crew practised their lifeboat drill in the form of a mock launching alternating their choice of these two craft. On this occasion the starboard boat's descent was halted before its keel touched the water. "Unless we drill whilst in dock the boat is not floated," was Green's answer when later I queried the 'dry' launching. Although our ship's progress had been severely muted, Brazendale held steerage-way throughout the exercise. Had, under these conditions, the boat been dunked its two occupants would have tasted more than the fresh-water that was carried aboard.

Once proved that the launching mechanism was fully serviceable, the sea skimming lifeboat with its skeletal crew had to be hauled by hand winch back to deck level. Greasers and stewards, engineers and cooks, seamen and navigators — paint-stained overalls mixed together with navy-blue worsted — as every possible permutation of crew took turns at cranking the low-geared two-man apparatus.

When the boat was finally inched back to its davits, much of the urgency had dissipated. Lighted-hearted ridicule was flung around as breathless personnel discarded their restrictive lifejackets and flopped against the rails. Cigarettes were lit up and the occasion relaxed into an unpremeditated outdoor social gathering.

Why, on such an advanced ship, was there no powered recovery system for the lifeboat?

It had long been secured inboard and the ship returned to its normal gait when, whilst on the bridge, I questioned Peter Green about the afternoon's event.

"I suppose lifeboats are only intended to go in one direction — it is getting them away smoothly that counts. In this direction it must be totally independent of all the ships's power systems; so in terms of recovery it is naturally likewise independent."

While I accompanied the chief officer on watch he remarked that we were exactly six days and one thousand nine hundred miles out of Hull. We were now scheduled to be docked at Purfleet for early Sunday morning. For the moment however the long low profile of Gotland provided a continuous source of interest three miles over to port. We had been cruising in company with this large island's western seaboard since late afternoon. At first it had appeared as a slender strip of land at the very edge of the sea. But gradually as our ship slogged closer to the shore, it became possible, through the glasses, to pick up something of the island's fascination.

Gotland is eighty miles in length and over thirty miles wide, it is the most easterly province of Sweden but in character remains a separate entity. Stemming back thousands of years, its illustrious history would fill many chapters. During the Middle Ages it was the greatest trading place in Northern Europe. Visby, its capital, was accepted as one of the major cities in the world. Largely controlled by German merchants, the community gained wealth comparable to that of London or Paris. At the time Visby had a population of around 40,000, which is nearly double that of today. Within the defensive line of its walls, the rich merchants built no less than sixteen well-proportioned churches. Throughout the island there are still in use ninety or so elaborate churches that date from that golden era.

At one stage in history, Visby became the battleground of various Baltic powers. In 1361 the massacre of a Swedish army outside the city wall sparked off its decline as a trading haven. Consequently Gotland changed hands many times until, in 1645, it became finally sealed to the Swedish nation.

Present-day Gotland enjoys a flourishing tourist industry. Its extensive coastline embraces thirty sandy beaches, some are remote quiet coves backed by dark green pine forests, others have camping sites that reach down to the water's edge. But the main attraction is Visby itself. Ranking among the most interesting and well-preserved medieval cities in Europe, it is a place of many traditional and cultural attractions. The fairy-tale city walls still display an almost unbroken fortification some two miles in length and sport thirty-seven towers. The gothic cathedral within is the island's largest ecclesiastical structure. The island's climate is said to be milder and sunnier than that of the Swedish mainland. Claim of this is borne out by the profusion of fruits and plants that thrive there.

Snugly situated half-way along the western seaboard, Visby, from the decks of our ship, conveniently unveiled its medieval charm from behind a screen of limestone cliffs. Lit up by the evening sun was a vista of tall red-roofed houses, enbattled walls and literally above all the three-domed towers of its majestic cathedral. Fronting all this a picturesque harbour was thronged with all manner of colourful craft.

Gotland provided a compelling scene that steadily changed as the burdened 'Enterprise' ploughed southwards. Church spires and windmill towers broke the flat masses of skyline forests while at the foreshore undercut craggy cliffs gave way to a wide selection of tree-fringed coves and sandy beaches. At the latter stages of our Gotland journey, co-ordinating information from the chart table with use of binoculars, Peter Green and I were able to pick out the rocky islets of Lilla Karlso and Sotra Karlso nestling a mile or so off-shore. Apart from seeing the breeding grounds of huge colonies of guillemots and razorbills, privileged visitors there are likely to discover many uncommon plants wedged among the rocky outcrops.

By and by, as we pushed on towards the night, Gotland reluctantly slipped beyond a darkening horizon leaving us once more alone in a spacious sea lane.

Throughout my voyage I was served from all corners constant reminders of the severe winter conditions Baltic shipping has to face. In January and February ice usually grips the Baltic as far south as Gotland. Sometimes, in the hardest of winters, the sea can freeze over as far as the reaches of Copenhagen or Kiel Bay. I had listened to a whole string of stories covering the trauma of shipping in battle for survival against ice conditions; such as the time when the Finnish icebreaker 'Varma' rescued 'Baltic Jet' from the brink of being bowled over by an ever-advancing wall of pressure ice several miles south of Helsinki. Or the occasion when having been in collision with the powerful breaker 'Tarmo,' the entire crew of a badly damaged ''Baltic Sprite' narrowly escaped being stranded for the winter at Finland's northernmost port of Kemi. There was talk of pilots skiing or motoring over the ice in order to reach incoming vessels — of crewmen walking across a deserted wilderness from a stranded ship to the shore — of times when having struggled for endless days to reach the Finnish coast, stores were exchanged between neighbouring icebound vessels by use of sledges, freshwater systems had gone solid and the accommodation blackened by rimed windows and port-holes.

Most of the dialogue was issued from the indelibly etched memories of the crew's more senior citizens, for, in the main, the tales dated back to the 50's and 60's when U.B.C. had a considerable fleet of small conventional freighters. Representing the younger blood aboard, the stories from Bernard Elworthy, Paul Davey or George Hall were restricted to the 70's when the advent of the larger ro-ro ships and introduction of more effective

'Baltic Enterprise' locked in Baltic pressure ice. Photograph by Chief Officer Peter Green.

135

Ice on foredeck after pounding through Baltic gale. Note rails running across top of picture.

On arrival at Helsinki, it was estimated that the ship was carrying 400 tons of ice.

137

icebreakers had lessened the degree of combat against the northern winters.

Not as if the elements were any more benevolent towards modern ships. Like against like, both types of vessels have faced the same cruel conditions. Yet, where the soaring high sides of ro-ro ships lift the crew and their accommodation way above and out of contact with the frozen surface, those travelling through ice-covered waters aboard a deeply laden conventional freighter are sat low and physically surrounded by jagged floes that have been thrust upwards by the ship's forward progress. When in this situation, the visual aspect alone falls nothing short of dramatic.

To round off a lengthy bout of 'ice talk' on that seventh night at sea, John Gunning delivered photographic evidence of the Baltic's potentially unyielding winter grip. The few who drifted from the smoke room's comfortable armchairs to the second engineer's darkened cabin saw, projected on to a white sheeted bulkhead, colour slides taken aboard 'Baltic Enterprise' herself the previous winter. Though the ship had a fully ice-strengthened hull and a theoretical potential of breaking through a crust of up to one metre thick, the pictures revealed her uncompromisingly blocked within a vast frozen arena.

Stage by stage the slides illustrated how on her way north, 'Enterprise' had scraped, smashed, jolted and eventually stopped in the most solid ice mass encountered in her Baltic ferrying history.

"At first the sensation was that of running into a crusty reef that gave way to our seemingly remorseless momentum. Then as the ice thickened and closed in, one noticed marked changes in the ship's attitude. Unfamiliar sounds became considerably louder and more frequent; at the same time her progress became hindered and fell into an irregular pattern. Over the side, twenty feet below the weather deck, the massive ice slabs being lifted by the bow progressively dropped back on themselves and crashed in rugged peaks against the ship's hull. With attendant jolting the noises took on a melée of scraping, crashing and hollow banging that one would expect to hear if the ship were being driven a cross a boulder-strewn bottom Sometimes the ship would be drawn to a halt. Here it was necessary to back-track down our own self-carved channel then charging at a full 'ten ahead' to meet the ice with all available force."

John Gunning's commentary ran in sequence with a series of high quality transparencies that had been taken from the upper decks of the ship.

"Eventually we arrived at a situation where the buckled ice surface began to close in behind us. Soon this was to put an end to the ramming technique so despite all efforts we became ice-bound forty miles or so short of Helsinki."

'Enterprise' was not alone in this predicament for in the winter sunlight the camera had picked out a varied assortment of shipping littering the ice at all angles over an area covering several square miles.

Even after being released by one of the efficient Finnish icebreakers, the large ro-ro's problems were not concluded — her liberal 73 foot beam proved to be an unprescribed encumbrance in the narrow closing channel carved by the rescue breaker and a great deal of strenuous bludgeoning was further required before she reached her goal.

There were also shots taken during the same term of events of rescued coasters and the like lashed with bow to the stern of the attendant icebreaker. Sailing in tandem the coaster's engine, though having minimal effect, was adding to the breaker's cause.

The picture show highlighted a completely adverse view of the Baltic to that which the ongoing voyage had revealed. Yet it held a compelling impact — one to which I responded by vowing to return one winter and sample for myself.

CHAPTER TWELVE

When choosing a course on which to sail between the Baltic and North Seas, a sea captain has three principal options. In brief these are namely the 'Great Belt,' the 'Sound' and the 'Kiel Canal.'

In deciding which route to take, he has to take into consideration the size of his ship, weather conditions, his time schedule and the fuel and pilotage costs to the owners. For those in command of the largest of ships that ply between these two seas, the 'Great Belt' is the only option available. When leaving the Baltic on this passage, he steers his ship between the Danish islands of Fyn and Zealand, then continues north through the Kattegat to Skagen and the 'Skaw.' In distance this is the longest of the three routes, but its straits provide the deepest and widest channel. Of the 'Sound,' the journey we have already covered, it is worth mentioning that being limited to carrying ships of no more than 7.5 metres draught, it is the most restrictive of the three routes.

Thirdly the Kiel Canal is the most favoured route for sea traffic movements between the Baltic ports and those located around the southern half of the North Sea — and indeed for most shipping heading for wider horizons through the English Channel. Effectively the Canal clips approximately 280 sea miles off such a voyage so, when considering present-day fuel costs, it presents a most attractive proposition. However on face value the saving in passage time is nothing like so great. Shipping using the 53-mile long Canal is restricted to a maximum speed of eight knots; thus it takes between seven and eight hours to complete the average passage. Compared to a fair-weather passage around the 'Skaw,' the saving in time can be as small as two hours. On the other hand, when gales rage across the waters of Northern Denmark, which in winter they often do, the Canal becomes an ongoing attraction from every angle. Added to the savings in fuel and time is the prospect of an eight-hour respite from angular seas.

Though we had been enjoying fair weather on our homeward voyage through the Baltic, Gerry Brazendale had elected to travel the Kiel Canal to effect the very shortest passage to the Thames. This was in no way an unusual decision for, though as Master he had the authority to choose the course his ship would take, it was regular practice for ships on the Finanglia operation inward and outward from the Purfleet base to use the Canal.

Geographically the Canal lies entirely within the boundaries of West Germany. It severs the low-lying neck of land that ultimately supports the Danish mainland — known as Jutland. The waterway follows a wavering course in a general N.E./S.W. direction. Specifically it links the south-west corner of the Baltic at Kiel Bay with the northern shore of the River Elbe three-quarters of the distance downstream from Hamburg to the North Sea. From a passenger's point of view the Kiel passage was an added bonus to the voyage. Breaking half-way across the homeleg it came as a timely relief to a three-day seascape.

Having overnight hauled progressively southwards we had passed the Olands Sodra Grund Lighthouse (known as 'Old Sod' to our navigators) and then briefly back-tracked our outward course between the Swedish mainland and Bornholm Island. From then onwards, throughout the morning, 'Enterprise' had been held on a south-westerly heading making for the extremities of the Southern Baltic.

Though the sea state had been slight, offering our ship a smooth carefree run, it had become increasingly more populated. None the least significant among the miscellany of ships we met or joined forces with along that latter stage of our Baltic voyage was a flotilla of West German naval gunboats. Numbering eight in all these identical craft sped close by our port-side heading, in arrow-straight line astern, purposefully towards the open sea. At the time our ship was being navigated along a closely buoyed channel that carried us almost westward through the Fehmarn Belt. To the north these straits were fringed by the shores of the Danish island of Lolland while to the south and beyond our port-side rail lay Puttgarden — a village on the German Fehmarn Island and a strategic point of the Belt ferry link.

Two hours later, thirty-five miles on and approaching mid-afternoon, our unerring pace was briefly curtailed when, at Kiel Lighthouse, we were brought to a near halt to take on the Kiel Pilot. His presence on the bridge was ultimately established and under his guidance we quickly resumed our progress towards the inviting spread of Kiel Bay (Kieler Forde). It was a bright expanse of water gaily punctuated with groups of multi-coloured sailed yachts and dinghies. The very fact that Kiel Bay was chosen as the venue for the 1972 Olympic sailing regattas illustrates the attraction these waters hold to international yachtsmen. A splendid new marina with berthing facilities for 800 craft was constructed to stage the event — this exclusive harbour was pin-pointed by a forest of masts over to starboard as our ship slid further into the inviting mouth of the Bay.

Shortly afterwards we were in more confined waters on a heading of 195 degrees and making a sedate ten knots. Having closed in, the shores revealed a scene varying from charming sea-edge holiday villages backed by soft green woodland on the east bank to unobtrusive shipyards and a helicopter base on the west side. It was in company with that more commercialised west shore that the deep water channel led us. It not only served the Canal with a continuous stream of traffic, it was also the main arterial route to the bustling port of Kiel.

Kiel itself is a city of some 270,000 inhabitants and capital of the State of Schleswig-Holstein. It straggles abundantly around the head of the tideless twelve-mile 'Forde' influentially displaying a pulsating activism. Capitalising on its natural harbour location, Kiel has developed to become one of Germany's main industrial centres. As a port it facilitates for every type of freight, is the terminal for numerous ferry services and is a popular port of call for Baltic cruise liners.

But the thrusting centre of Kiel was not for us. Half-way along the shore that would have carried us there the pilot had the ship brought to a near halt. We had arrived at Holtenau, the starting place for our Canal journey. For a while, 'Enterprise' ambled on the sunlit water in an undecided manner — likewise did the small coaster that had followed us a cable astern on our passage across the Bay. Our wait was simply an execution of the highway code — there were traffic-lights on the shore that clearly indicated that we were not to proceed. They were in favour of a variegated string of commercial shipping that was soon to emerge from the Canal channel. For a time the scene was that of a High Street junction for astern of us two more vessels had now joined the queue. The marshalling was conducted under strict control and with the passing of the last and largest vessel we were able to proceed.

The odd assortment of ships that were now heading seawards down the Bay had been released from one of the huge locks that straddled across the head of the Canal — this particular lock-pit was now vacant and offered an open invitation to our lumbering ro-ro.

"Hard to starboard!" I heard the pilot command the helmsman; he was directing operations from inside the bridgehouse. Gerry Brazendale had moved out to the port wing control position — it would be he and he alone who would present 'Enterprise' to the lock.

At Holtenau there were two pairs of locks — large and small, respectively new and old. We were destined for the 'north' pit of the larger pair. When using the term large I would indicate that being over 1,000 feet in length and almost 150 feet in breadth each of these locks would theoretically consume four ships of 'Enterprise's' dimensions! Being free to enter an empty pit of such enormity, Brazendale was able to manoeuvre at will — unlike the tight situation I had witnessed at Hull a week earlier, I likened this event to negotiating the Upper Thames locks with a motor cruiser. Subsequently we were quickly moored in the lock with our port-side lying at the centre island quay.

Although the origins of the Kiel Canal date back to the early 19th century when the territory belonged to the Danes, the waterway that exists today was a product of German ingenuity during the period between 1888 and 1895. Officially opened on January 21st, 1895, by Emperor Wilhelm II, it was duly named the Kaiser-Wilhelm Canal. It was soon an established route highly beneficial to the exchange of goods between nations along the Baltic coasts and their world-wide trade partners. Such was the impact of the new North Sea/Baltic route that as early as 1899 it enjoyed an annual traffic flow of 26,000 ships. Realising the strategic importance of the Canal the Germans were quick to extend its potential. Between 1904 and 1914 it was both deepened and widened; thus it was capable of carrying the large warships that they were energetically building prior to World War I.

Due to damage inflicted by the continuous heavy volume of traffic, a massive programme of improvements commenced in 1965.

The Kiel Canal (known in West Germany as the Nord-Ostee-Kanal) is open to shipping all day and night throughout the year. Being the most used sea-linking canal in the world, it is estimated that on a yearly average one vessel passes through every eight minutes. Charges for ships (canal dues, pilotage fees, etc.) are based on gross tonnage. Due to the rapid rise of fuel oil prices in the late 70's, more and more ship owners have turned to the Canal as an effective means of containing overheads.

The Nord-Ostee-Kanal Annual Report 1980 reads:

"The 1980 result in gross tonnage of 93 million GRT was an absolute record since the existence of the Kiel Canal. 93,058,549 GRT were produced by 56,677 vessels. This is an increase of 8.6% over the previous year. The trend towards the larger and more economical vessels which has been observed for years continues.

"Total goods traffic increased from 59,726,578 tons (1979) to 62,082,416 tons (1980) an increase of 3.9%.

"The annual traffic average on the Kiel Canal was 155 vessels per day. The busiest day was 12th August with 233 vessels, the quietest day was 29th December with 40 vessels.

"As has been the case in the past year's annual average, Monday was registered in 1980 as the quietest weekday with 139 vessels, followed by Sunday with 143 vessels. As for the remaining days, a constant increase was ascertained as the week progressed. Saturday once again proved to be the busiest day of the week with 178 sluicings."

Situated at Holtenau lock-side are the offices of the United Baltic Corporation GmbH. As agents for shipping using the Canal, U.B.C. have been operative at Kiel since 1946. Currently U.B.C. handle the documentation of 30% of all Kiel Canal traffic; in doing so they employ some 37 people based both at Holtenau and at Brunsbuttel. They have a further office at Kiel Harbour from where cargo shipments are organised. Since 1978 the operation has been managed by Mr. Ian Gibson to whom I am indebted for supplying literature about the Canal.

We shared the lock with four other craft — two coasters of around 500 gross tons, a Polish freighter of similar size to ourselves (which to my amazement had such a surplus of crew that no fewer than fourteen men attended the forward mooring deck) and finally a cruiser-yacht around thirty feet in length that had gingerly crept into the pit when all the 'hardware' had been securely moored. In close company with towering commercial ships, its white fibreglass hull looked as vulnerable as an egg in a box of sledge-hammers.

Once the seaward gates had closed and the lock began to fill, our short break at Holtenau was almost at an end. At the quayside was a small shop and post office. It was there specially for the convenience of seamen from ships passing through the locks. I watched three of our own seamen dash from its doors and along the scrupulously tidy precincts to the rising bulk of the ship where their companions were continually adjusting the accommodation ladder to the new level. Slow service was one commodity this shop could not afford to put on offer!

When level with the expanse of canal water that magically opened up ahead, 'Enterprise' regained her true height. From the 'monkey island,' Bob and Ruth Turnbull and I took in an observation platform vista much dissimilar to the deep-blue circle of the ocean. And in saying that it was a landscape far removed from my expectations. Up to that time the very

High-level road bridges at Holtenau. Beyond: locks and spacious waters of Kiel Bay.

words 'shipping canal' released an image of a satanic trench with no more than tall chimneys and cooling towers for scenery. The chance of voyaging the Kiel had only arisen shortly before the trip; consequently, I had done no groundwork.

Holtenau appeared as a most pleasant residential suburb of Kiel. Amid the lush green cover of the northern bank's broad-leafed trees were many avenues of fine houses. It was a place that spelled prosperity — not the least in the tidy commercial premises that lined the Canal's southern shore. These were chiefly bases of the internationally known oil companies. At their quays, ships could conveniently berth and re-bunker before heading back to sea. At the lock-side were railed promenades from which the general public could while away an hour or so watching the ships go by. The immediate area was neatly lawned and gardened. In particular I noted the harbour-master's offices directly on the lock gates; set within its grassed frontage was a landscaped mosaic of the West German national emblem. In similar vein on the opposite shore the U.B.C. offices were fronted by a wide patio that also overlooked the Canal's endless activity.

Underway, at a most dignified pace, we were soon to pass beneath two closely linked high-level road bridges. They were the first of seven imposing bridge structures that at various stages carry both road and rail over the fifty-three mile waterway. The minimum height of these bridges above the water is 137 feet — the maximum height allowed for the masts of ships is 132 feet.

Onwards from the Holtenau bridges we cruised slowly into the heart of the German countryside. If not spectacular the scenery held a strange fascination — the unlikely event of a large sea-going vessel journeying between green fields where cattle grazed, wooded hillsides in which rabbits scurried and parklands where families picnicked had suddenly turned into reality. All credit to the German authorities for making an amenity of the Canal side. Down at its cobbled banks young and old sat fishing, others strolled along miles of well-surfaced towpaths or came just to feed the ducks and swans that bobbed on the gently rolling wake of passing ships. Inns and restaurants boasted gardens or patios that reached down to the water's edge. Car parks were at regular intervals, sometimes in woodland clearings that offered an unhindered view of the passing scene. Along the route people often gave a friendly wave, a greeting to which the small group on 'Enterprise's' high decks cheerfully responded.

Always there were ships. Astern those that had shared the lock kept at a respectable distance. From ahead came an irregular flow of variegated tonnage. Mostly they were smaller vessels than our own — tugs, barges, naval craft and pleasure boats — more common than any were the deep-laden coasters inevitably registered at Hamburg or Antwerp.

One of these hard-working vessels still bore the scars of the long-past winter in as much as the lower half of her hull was completely stripped of paint.

"Ice scrubbed," an equally astonished Peter Green called up from the port wing.

145

Infrequently we met up with larger ships. On these occasions great caution was exercised. Large ships moving in close company are known to attract each other like magnets. Likewise two vessels of large displacement passing in a confined channel can create a massive tidal surge — one that could seriously erode the Canal's precious banks. To eliminate the possibility of untoward happenings, passing places are provided at eleven selected points along the route. In conjuction there is a tightly controlled signalling system, directions from which all craft must obey.

Having travelled at a subdued $7\frac{1}{2}$ knots for more than two hours (often in company with horse-riders, cyclists or joggers), we were confronted by high pyloned traffic lights that flashed continually at red. Our Canal pilot had 'Enterprise' brought into the starboard side lay-by at that point and held hard against the high dolphins there. 'Antoni Granuszewski' was the name spread across the Polish-registered freighter that eventually rounded a distant tree-shaded bend. Though of considerable tonnage, she was not the most impressive of vessels to be served when having waited several minutes in high expectation. Crew was something these Polish ships were not deficient in. Above the two penguins painted on her lofty hull, the rails were lined by more than one hundred men — "Some kind of merchant training ship" Peter Green advised his enquiring passengers.

For the record, the Canal informative literature indicates that the maximum permissible length for a ship using the waterway is 771 feet, in breadth 106 feet. The largest ship en-transit on the Canal in 1980 was the 36,265 gross ton Greek bulk carrier 'Mount Paranassos'; she was in ballast en route from Leningrad to Hamburg.

"It's like dining on a slow-moving railcar," our young American travelling companions commented as from the dinner table we looked out over a steadily changing rural scene. How right they were; had we been seated in the dining car of a German train the general aspect of the neighbouring farmsteads, thatched cottages and individually designed houses would have been no different. But the novelty of sailing overland meant little to our mariner hosts. They had voyaged the Kiel seemingly a thousand times; to them the green fields through the port side windows were just pictures on the walls. Inevitably the conversation would revert to the turn-round at Purfleet, the port engine gearcase, the latest 'test match' score or the weather.

In this respect Brazendale and Green had shared the dinner-hour between the bridge and the table. They had brought with them news of impending bad weather. Away from the two spells of fog and rain around the Finnish coast we had, over the past week, become somewhat complacent about the climatic conditions. Now, with a depression rapidly approaching the 'high' over northern Europe, a gale warning had been issued for all U.K. sea areas — Germany Bight, Humber and Thames included.

There was a strong possibility that, at the 'eleventh hour' of the voyage, we would sail directly into the teeth of south-westerly winds of force eight or nine.

"Should nicely meet it in the Elbe estuary." Having studied the radio officer's report, Brazendale blandly scribed his calculations to five enquiring passengers.

"Summer gales are not an unknown quantity in the North Sea but, if it's any consolation, unlike winter storms they seldom last. From November onwards north-easterlies can blow with no respite for more than a week on end. Often we have battled into them across to Skagen or Kiel on our outward track to Finland, had a comparatively smooth Baltic passage but then re-engaged the very same North Sea gale on the homeward leg."

But at that time, despite the warning of gales, our ship seemed over-poweringly large and, as steady as a rock, she purred nonchalantly onwards along the iron-smooth canal fairway. Through a passenger's eyes, such ideas of her being pitched around in impetuous waters within a matter of hours seemed totally unrealistic. Complacent we were — it would take more than a slip of paper bearing a met forecast to interfere with our snug summer world!

Approaching the half-way stage of our Kiel Canal journey, we passed through Rendsburg. Of 50,000 inhabitants this was the only place of substance encountered between the terminals of the Canal. Though essentially an inland town, Rendsburg capitalises on its waterside location — shipbuilding was an industry much in evidence from the decks of our ro-ro. In this direction I was informed that it was at these yards that many of U.B.C.'s past conventional ships had been built and the company's ro-ro 'Goya' was lengthened.

Nearer the town we looked down on quays and wharfes at which were moored several coasters, petroleum carriers and freighters that I suspected were hauling grain. We travelled through built-up areas where attractive steep-roofed houses with observation patios overlooked the water, where roadways carried cars and lorries close and parallel with the ship and areas where tree-fringed promenades gave residents the opportunity to closely view the Canal's endless traffic flow. There was a modern styled hotel. Through its large picture windows, diners looked out at 'Enterprise's' slow-moving bulk in awe. Simultaneously there were guests watching from bedroom balconies; had we been a little closer we could have reached out to shake them by the hand.

Even more interesting than the waterside buildings at Rendsburg were the various spectacular means of linking the two shores thereabouts. First there had been high-speed traffic flying over our heads on a leggy concrete bridge that carried the Hamburg/Flensburg autobahn. Its angular main span had taken one straight and slender leap directly over our shimmering path. Within a mile was one of the twelve selected points where small ferry boats carry cars and passengers free of charge (so I understand) to and fro between either bank. Close to the hub of Rendsburg was a most unusual steel railway viaduct. To gain sufficient height to cross the canal, it spiralled through a complete 360 degrees. This massive loop, somewhere in the order of a mile in diameter and gradually rising above the town, looked as though it belonged to an oversized fun-fair. Not only did it whisk Kiel-bound trains high over the canal but it also carried road vehicles at a much lower level. Suspended beneath the main steel span was a moving platform that travelled smoothly between the two banks several feet above the water. Obviously, having to cross such a busy waterway on a regular basis, the transporter's journey had to be carefully timed. I noticed that while 'Enterprise' was beneath the bridge and directly abeam of the platform it had already commenced its 550-foot trek. By the time our ship had cleared the bridge, the transporter with a load of ten cars was directly astern and half-way across the canal. Soon the ship trailing our wake was level with the bridge but by then the suspended platform had reached its destination — split-second timing to say the least!

Finally, past the south-western boundary of Rendsburg, a deep gorge had been carved out of the landscape at either side and at right-angles to the canal. Within the cleft of this disturbed land ran a broad road that sped traffic deep beneath our liquid road. The tunnel was a product of the 1960's and carried yet another trunk route between Hamburg and Denmark.

Had I not been out on deck at the time, the ship's brief halt at a point west of Rendsburg would have gone unnoticed. We had arrived at the mid-distance mark and here abeam to starboard was the main canal pilot exchange station — a building that resembled one of the more modern and sophisticated railway signal boxes.

Since Holtenau we had been navigated by a specialised canal pilot who had brought aboard his own helmsman. There had been no disrespect aimed at the ability of 'Enterprise's' own deck crew — canal regulations demand that ships of her calibre engage both pilot and helmsmen for the journey. Needless to say this was not a complete take-over. Our watch-keeping officer was on the bridge at all times and whenever there was any close manoeuvring to be carried out Brazendale invariably appeared from the shadows.

At this half-way point, the Holtenau pilot left the ship to be replaced by a further pilot who was to guide us to Brunsbuttel on the northern bank of the River Elbe.

A fussing pilot boat was quickly discarded from our ship's towering walls and again we headed serenely out across the northern neck of West Germany. On this leg it appeared that the further we travelled the more flat and monotonous the countryside became. But by now the day was ageing and gathering clouds brought a premature darkness over the scene — navigation lights glowing, we moved on towards the night.

Indoors the quiet of the boat deck level had been lifted through an unusually well attended social hour in the smoke room. Several of the younger officers had taken a communal sauna bath and their ignited faces warmed the bar-side scene. There was little doubt that the congenial mood had been raised through a configuration of ongoing circumstances — the relaxed pace of the ship — the seemingly appropriate tunes from Carl's guitar and for some the prospect of taking leave on arrival in the U.K.

I too began to think of our landfall but not specifically in a euphoric way. Unlike these crewmen, I was on leave, a leave that was now drawing nearer

148

and nearer to an end with every mile the ship sailed. Saturday was but an hour away; in a little more than two days time I was due back in harness. All too soon I would be again lingering at the sea-shore en route for work, repairing cycle punctures, mowing the grass and washing the car. Very shortly I would have to step off this floating steel box and its timeless world of incessant ferrying, such a time when I would be compelled to physically turn my back upon the ship and her crew. Yet I had a mandate to transcribe the experience aboard 'Enterprise' for the enlightenment and hopefully the enjoyment of others; therefore I would in no way be deserting her.

Thirty minutes past midnight and our Kiel Canal journey was over. Brunsbuttel's outer lock gates had retracted to release 'Baltic Enterprise' onto an inky black channel that curved gently away to starboard. Overhead a solid cloud cover blanketed out the night sky — it was dark and, moreover, there was a hint of rain in the gathering wind that plucked at my clothes. On rounding the beacons that marked the outer limit of the channel we started to roll laboriously. This was the River Elbe — at this point over one mile wide and twenty-five miles from the sea.

The lights of Brunsbuttel had glowed abundantly, radiating a scene far remote from that described by John Garvey, when as a lad he had first sailed to the town.

"The War had just ended and the people here were on the verge of starvation. It was a pathetic sight — they came down to the ships carrying their last possessions to barter or simply beg for food."

But today's affluent Brunsbuttel was dropping astern and now, in response to the pilot's calculated orders, our ship had been steered to the buoyed channel that would lead us to the sea. Once more the engines had broken into full cry and the ship's inevitable mood of urgency had been restored. Gale warnings apart we had embarked on a 400-mile haul across a stretch of notoriously inconsiderate water.

Before turning in, I tugged up my collar and took a lonely walk on the windswept deck. I watched the shore illuminations settle into the distance; a curtain had been drawn across the Canal and a 53-mile passage that had brought a new dimension to the voyage.

CHAPTER THIRTEEN

Daybreak, a reluctant July daybreak, with a spume-streaked sea that boiled incessantly into the hazy-grey horizon. The rain-laden south-westerly wind impelled an endless succession of white-capped waves into walls of aquatic fury. Amid this menacing ocean, 'Baltic Enterprise' pitched and rolled in a monotonous sequence of precipitation. Such was the geometry of this cauldron's surface that I likened it to a boundless estate of steep-roofed houses — and in this context we plunged headlong from roof-tops to gardens in consistent sickening falls that left the stomach churning twenty feet above.

With each successive surge our burdened ro-ro buried her bow deep into the base of a salt-sea furrow. Then, while still shuddering through the impact, she laboriously elevated her rounded bulwarks through a maelstrom of bleached white liquid until such times they angled to the grey-lined sky. Simultaneously 452 feet away, her stern settled into the trough with quavering proclamation of burrowing screws. With engines at near maximum power and being held tight ahead by her auto-pilot, 'Enterprise' was obliged to forge directly into the teeth of the gale. This blatant attack upon the elements induced violent eruptions of crippled water to sweep high over and across the container-laden weather deck. Together with the wind-driven rain, a desultory fog of sea-spray partially shrouded the superstructure tower. The prospect through the salt-rimed bridgehouse windows at dawn that late July day was one of a frenzied climatic revolt. If mid-summer madness were to be defined then surely this was it.

Sleep had not been a forthcoming commodity. The ever-increasing movement of the ship was gradually spreading each and every loose item across the cabin carpet. My 'pad' had become alive with unfamiliar sounds. Creaks and groans were cast from unclosed wardrobe doors and irritated deck-head panel seams, window blinds snapped continuously against the glass and my dressing-gown swished through an ever-widening arc on its bulkhead peg. Before the cabin was reduced to a state of turmoil I had rolled from beneath the sheets and unsteadily stowed my things.

This was no longer the luxuriously secure world to which I had blame-lessly become accustomed. With top clothes over my pyjamas I swayed across the brightly lit alleyway towards the stairway to the bridge. I was not alone. Awake for his early watch stint, John Gunning had also adopted the same inquisitive state of mind. Together we discreetly entered the swaying bridgehouse.

Moving around in the half-light were three navigators. Bernard Elworthy, whose watch had fifteen minutes to run, Peter Green, whose sleep had also been disturbed through the excessive motion, and the Master, who had not left the bridge since Brunsbuttel.

According to the chart that Elworthy was busily pencilling up to date, the last three hours had yielded no more than forty miles. Having passed the German fishing town of Cuxhaven to port one hour earlier, we had now put twelve miles of the raging water between our rolling stern and the

150

mouth of the River Elbe. Thirty miles to the south the coastline contour swept down to Bremerhaven and the River Weser, northwards and twenty-five miles of ocean away was the tiny island of Heligoland. Our course was 265 degrees. The wind was attacking from ten or more points to port.

Brazendale and Green moved between the radar glow and streaming windows in pensive silence. Grim-faced, Brazendale was monitoring the ship's attitude to the steep seas — the angle of roll to him was the most important factor. Accepting the fact that we were pitching more or less directly into the weather, he knew us to be on a satisfactory course. However, often a rogue wave would persuade the ship to heel steeply — first to starboard then back with a rush to an even greater angle to port. 'Enterprise' was a ship with a towering hull structure; moreover her height above the water was further increased by the double-decked containers she was carrying on her weather deck. Many of these were empty but nonetheless together they totalled a considerable weight, effectually lifting the ship's centre of gravity. Brazendale was more than aware of this — this is what concerned him.

Yet to these mariners the gale appeared as a temporary problem. They did not seem to look upon it as a long-term prospect — "Blow itself out by mid-day," I heard, exchanged between them. Additionally, once further away from the coast they expected the short steep seas to open up. They knew these waters and the influence a westerly gale has upon them. In turn they knew their ship and her capabilities. To the landsman the beating she was taking was severe; to them this was just another gale among the many hundreds the ship had encountered. It was far from a happy occasion but there had been many worse — far worse.

Despite their impressive bulk, ro-ro ships are no less vulnerable to severe conditions than any other. While wedged in the bridgehouse starboard corner uncomfortably scribbling my account of the ongoing situation, my thoughts went back to November 1977 and the fate of the 4,500 gross ton Hull-registered ro-ro 'Hero.' Not many miles north-west of our position, this one-time Queen Elizabeth Dock stable companion of 'Enterprise' lay on the bed of the North Sea under 100 feet of water. At the time of the disaster, 'Hero' was operating on her regular service en route from Esbjerg to Grimsby carrying 3,650 tons of unitised cargo valued at £3 million. Having set sail from the Danish port in the evening of 11th November, the vessel was soon battling with a force eight gale. Just after midnight she encountered a violent storm with heavy rain, nil visibility, sheet lightning and a wind gusting force ten. Like all ships that regularly ply the North Sea, 'Hero' was not unaccustomed to heavy weather (twice during her five years of ferrying between Denmark and the U.K. she had limped to the Humber listing badly through shifted cargoes); however on this occasion she began to ship water.

In common with all ro-ro vessels, 'Hero' was a hard-pressed ship. The previous year she had left an Amsterdam dry-dock having been lengthened by the addition of a new 70-foot midships section. This modification had increased her cargo capacity by 40%. Since that time, 'Hero' had been subjected to a rigorous work schedule through which her managers had requested a three months postponement of her annual survey.

Initially the ingress of sea-water was traced to worn rubber seals around ill-fitting stern doors but soon it was discovered that there were other leaks. The deck crew were successful in plugging a three foot long crack in her port quarter but this did little to improve the situation. Now hove-to and being battered by winds of force 11, 'Hero' took on a severe starboard list. Operating at 50 tons per hour, her pumps were unable to cope with the deluge that was progressively flooding the engine room and the lower cargo deck. Apart from the ingress at her steeply dipping stern, more water was thought to be coming from a split seam underneath the ship.

At 10.30 a.m. on 12th November, the Master, in fear of a capsize, sent out an S.O.S. which was immediately answered by three vessels in the near vicinity — the motor ship 'Valerie,' the Canadian frigate 'Huron' and no less than the formidable 'Tor Britannia.' Of 'Hero's' twenty-seven crew and three passengers, nine were lifted from her upper decks by helicopter to 'Tor Britannia,' six were lifted to 'Huron' and fourteen in liferafts were taken aboard the 'Valerie.' One man died having suffered a heart attack while climbing the shipside ladder. 'Hero' sank by the stern some twenty-eight hours after being abandoned.

The report from a ten-day formal investigation into the sinking disclosed that although 'Hero' was unseaworthy in other respects, it was only the water seeping through her stern doors that caused the disaster. Blame for her fate was "in part" caused by the "wrongful act or default" of her owners who failed to maintain the stern doors. The Wreck Commissioner concluded: "Having regard to the hard use of these doors, the likelihood of damage and their vulnerability to the seas, a reasonable standard of maintenance required a system whereby careful attention was paid to their condition and any leakage reported and tested. No such system existed."

At breakfast time and four hours on we were punching a course of 252 degrees. This carried us directly into wind and parallel with the Frisian Island chain. Respectively from east to west this string of twenty or so islets come under the West German and Dutch flags. With the day now fully awake, the prospect through the salt-sprayed windows appeared less hostile than at dawn. The rain had ceased and a smattering of sunlit patches appeared amid the windswept clouds. Above and beyond the spray shroud that periodically fused from festoons of bow-smashed water, the sea surface showed as an oscillating circle of blue-grey and white. A more defined wave frequency had been established and now one could begin to predict the ship's motion — yet, despite the brighter outlook, this motion was no less severe.

Within the accommodation block, familiar surroundings were seen at unfamiliar angles. The imbalance sensation was acute; in effect a feeling of another power dominating over us. Now and then unclosed cabin doors would crash to and fro and, for the first time during the voyage, one had to carefully plan each and every move between strategic points. As the ship plummeted into a trough, the fore-aft alleyways dropped forward to the creaking accompaniment of protesting panelwork. While burrowing her bow into the oncoming mountain, a mild shudder ran the length of the hull. Simultaneously the ship's forward progress would be briefly arrested to the extent that one would be lurched forward as a standing passenger in a braking bus. Then as she steadily lifted her head to the wave crest, the carpeted deck would reverse its angle in the fashion of a fun-fair ride — a motion to which the unwary would sway drunkenly and grasp for support.

Needless to say it was not a situation that stimulated the appetites of non-seafarers. With the absence of three of my travelling companions, the breakfast table was more forlorn than of late. For quite a while, Bob Turnbull and I sat alone nibbling lightly buttered toast and sipping dark coffee from crockery that clung to a dampened table cover. Of the few crew members that popped into the saloon that Saturday morning, Peter Green and John Gunning appeared to be alone in ordering a hearty breakfast. Until their arrival from early watch duties, the menu card had not been considered. On noticing our 'under par' performance at the ever-unlevelling table, they sympathetically advised "the best way to ward off seasickness is to eat well and keep active."

Up to then Bob and I had done little but lament over the unfortunate weather conditions.

"Had we not been diverted to West Finland we would have been alongside at Hull now," Bob had declared. How right he was. At the time, to us, the added visit to Turku and Mantyluoto had been a bonus but now the reality was that we were paying for it! Obviously the ship was going to arrive back at Hull two days later than originally intended. Here I had come to terms with the fact that on docking at Purfleet the following morning, my commitments were such that I had no alternative other than leave the ship and take the train north.

Later, in an effort to 'keep active,' I took up a standing invitation to visit the radio room. Considering the normal watch-keeping schedule aboard, Radio Officer Roy Caple had a job apart. Though like any other man aboard he was available for duty throughout the twenty-four hours, his normal working day was split into three periods — 08.00 to 12.00, 15.00 to 17.00 and 20.00 to 22.00. But more significant than his differing work schedule, Roy Caple was the only crew member who was not directly employed by U.B.C. All but the larger U.K. shipping lines contract their radio officers from specialised radio telegraphy companies. As an employee of Kelvin Hughes, Caple was one from a pool of qualified 'sparks' who were posted to wherever their services were contracted. Likewise was the equipment that he operated — this was installed in the ship by the Kelvin Hughes company on a 'rental' basis.

Roy Caple was a tall clean-cut young man with a clear determination to succeed in life. In this respect youth was on his side. For had we not been carrying a teenage pantry-boy, Caple, at twenty-two years of age, would have claimed to have been the youngest man aboard. Like the Master he hailed from Dorset. From leaving school he had taken a three-year course at Southampton Nautical College and qualified as radio officer at the first attempt. After completing a further six-month electronic course, he had secured a job at sea — a career that spanned a modest two years.

Taking the face of modern electronic equipment into consideration, the apparatus before him did not appear over complex. While 'Enterprise' bludgeoned her way across the North Sea, 'Sparks,' headphone clamped to his ear, pointed at the dial-littered consoles.

"More or less standard gear, V.H.F. — range thirty miles, M.F. with a maximum range of two-hundred miles, H.F. international Kelvin Hughes transmitter."

He also briefly outlined certain aspects of his duties — "Listening out for the ship's call-sign — possibly owners or agents withing to contact with orders, traffic lists, weather reports and forecasts, emergency signals and distress calls." With regard to emergency signals he told me of the regulation three-minute silence period 15-18 minutes and 45-48 minutes past every hour.

"If a vessel with a low-powered transmitter was in difficulties, the silence period allows him clear space and a greater chance of being heard."

As mentioned earlier, the radio room was located on the port side of the navigating bridgedeck directly abaft the bridgehouse. As the radio officer's living quarters were linked to his place of work, he was the only permanent resident at this deck level. To some degree this arrangement segregated him from the rest of the ship. Away from mealtimes I had seen little of Roy Caple. When our paths had crossed, I found him to be a source of up-to-the-minute information, particularly where the weather was concerned — today was no exception.

"Air pressure's rising again — wind backing southerly — down to force five by mid-afternoon. Should see some sun — get your deckchair booked!"

Though his last remark was somewhat presumptuous, the forecast proved to be near accurate. Around 14.30, feeling considerably more attuned to the ship's mode of riding the seas, I ventured out on deck. At first, clung to the after rail, I gazed over and afar of our swaying stern. Today the frothing wake that I had often seen linger for miles astern was quickly spread and dissipated amidst the melée of white-topped waves that had angrily challenged 'Enterprise's' progress. Then sneaking gingerly out to the port rail, I was hit by an unyielding wind that seemed determined to take the anorak off my back. But here the gripping manifestation was not so much of the power of the wind that ripped along the deck but the noise it created in doing so. Above, far above, the roar of the waves that crashed and banged against our high steel walls was the scream of the gale rushing through the stanchions, halyards and aerials that adorned the upperworks.

Improving though they were, conditions did not calm sufficiently to allow one out on deck for any length of time until nightfall. Therefore I utilised much of the afternoon and evening writing up my notes and making the rounds to express thanks to the crew for their co-operation over the past nine days. Though it was claimed my inquisitiveness had not

Alongside at Purfleet. Here the ship loads from a floating pontoon which is served from the shore by a link-span bridge (extreme left) (Skyfotos, Ashford, Kent).

155

been a hindrance I felt that there must have been times when I was wished well over the horizon.

Such was the last stage of my voyage aboard 'Baltic Enterprise.' With little to see except the occasional vessel tracing a darkening horizon and those aboard tired from the activity of the past twenty hours, the mood was more subdued than at any other time. Having myself spent much of the previous night out of the sheets, tiredness had not escaped me either. Hence after a couple of drinks in the company of Clive Buchan and George Hall, I followed the trend and turned in for an early night.

Purfleet lies on the North Bank of the Thames, approximately half-way between Tower Bridge and the river estuary near Southend. Having taken aboard the estuary pilot from a cutter at the Sunk Lightship and exchanged him for the river pilot off Gravesend all within the space of the early hours, 'Enterprise' had berthed at Purfleet's floating link-span in the glare of morning sunlight. Shortly after breakfast, all the noise and bustle of the turn-round began. The scene was little different to that described at the other ports of call during the past week.

For me it was time to leave. Sad not to be completing the circuit with the ship along the East Coast to Hull but glad of the 2,700 miles behind from which I had gleaned so much. All too soon amidst fleeting farewells and visits of Customs and Immigration Officers, the taxi that I was to share to town with the Turnbulls had arrived. Such was the hubbub around the ship and the shore that our departure went almost unnoticed.

Ironically I was not to know on taking a last glance to the ship's soaring grey and white structure through the taxi's rear window that I was to see her again the following day.

While wedged in a corner of the Hull-bound Inter-City, I suddenly remembered my tape recorder. A quick search through my luggage confirmed my fears. Through the hurried departure I had overlooked a final check through my cabin. The recorder had been packed in a dressing-table drawer for safety during the gale — it had not been used since. I contacted the ship from a public phone at Hull's Paragon Station. Within minutes the item had been found and at John Garvey's suggestion it was to be brought from Purfleet to Hull on the ship and handed over to the shore office. It would remain there until such times as I could collect it.

After the following day settling back to work, I made an early evening journey to Queen Elizabeth Dock. On pulling up there, the scene was much the same as on the day I had embarked. The Rotterdam-bound North Sea Ferries 'Norland' was once again entering the Humber from the lock, and, following, a loaded 'Baltic Enterprise' was scribing an arc in the dock water. She had hauled up from Purfleet overnight and throughout the day had taken aboard another consignment for Helsinki and Kotka.

I collected the stray recorder from the dockside office and made for the lock-pit in time to see 'Enterprise' make her entrance. There were new faces amongst the mooring deck crews and high up on the bridge wing — Gerry

Brazendale had been relieved of his charge at Purfleet, the others had changed over at Hull.

With all the usual care and precision, 'Enterprise' was duly locked through to the river. The Dockmaster's whistle gave the all-clear and her propellers bit furiously at the murky Humber. Her bow was swung round to head for the sea and another voyage had begun — yet another chapter in her log — it was Ro-Ro to Finland all over again.

PUBLICATIONS READ IN RESEARCH

'Scandinavia' by W. R. Mead and Wendy Hall.
'Finland' by Gladys Nichol.
'Gotland' by Arthur Spencer.
'Supership' by Noel Mostert.
'Seamanship' by T. F. Wickham.
'Lighthouses of England and Wales' by Derrick Jackson.
'Kotka' by Jukka Vehkasalo.
'The Hull Daily Mail.'
'Sea Breezes' magazine.
'City of Kingston upon Hull' by W. R. Watkinson.

AUTHOR'S NOTE

Shortly after compiling this book, I was informed that 'Baltic Enterprise' had been rescheduled onto a U.B.C. service between Middlesbrough and Aarhus, Denmark. She was replaced on the Finanglia service with U.B.C.'s latest and largest ro-ro vessel, the Finnish-built 'Baltic Eagle.' At this time of writing, 'Enterprise's' identical sister, 'Baltic Progress,' operates together with 'Baltic Eagle' on a slightly revised schedule to that described.

Regrettably it has to be reported that 'Baltic Enterprise' was ultimately sold to Yugoslavian interests and is now understood to operate in Mediterranean waters under the name of 'Klipa.'

BARRY MITCHELL,
Bridlington.
August, 1985.